# Summer of '49

## Hot Dogs, Hot Tamales and Number Two Tubs

*by*

# Charlie Bothuell

To Cliff W. P.
Friend For Life

Charlie "Chuck"
Bothwell
Aug 27
2010

# Summer of '49

## Hot Dogs, Hot Tamales and Number Two Tubs

*by*

# Charlie Bothuell

*Published by:*

**Joshua Tree Publishing**
1901 N. Roselle Road
Suite 800
Schaumburg, IL 60195

www.JoshuaTreePublishing.com

ISBN: 0-9710954-7-7

Printed in the United States of America

*This book is dedicated to*

*Aunt Lenore*

*First in our Family to graduate*
*Pontiac High School, 1937*

*She Saved Momma*

*Momma Saved Us*

*Thank You*

*This book is also dedicated to*

*Momma*

*Momma at 19 Years Old*

*She Saved Her Children*
*She Saved Herself*
*She Finally Believed in Herself*
*We Were Never Able to Tell Her How Much We Loved Her*
*But She Knew*

*Mickey and Nola Ruth*

# Table of Contents

## PART TWO: BASEBALL
## THE FEEL AND ESSENCE OF THE GAME

# PROLOGUE

This book was not inspired. It was not a burning, consuming passion that had to be fulfilled. It was something I had thought about, but never figured I'd get around to doing. At reunions and parties, friends often talk about their childhood and things they did. Everyone has special memories. And they even have different memories about the same events. Everybody would insist that his or her version of whatever was the real one. And someone would always say: "If you know so much, you should write about it. You were always the person who talked the most or the loudest."

Thus, this story is loosely woven, around the snap shots of one boy's questionable memory of the summer of 1949. The story is about what the writer and his family did.

Although there were probably a thousand black kids in all of the Saginaw Schools, there were a lot fewer eleven and twelve year olds. They all lived a different life, in different families, in the same town. And yet, they all shared and lived the same kind of life.

Most importantly, their families all agreed on what was right and wrong in a moral sense; whether they lived it or not. And everybody watched everybody's children in Saginaw, Michigan.

The skeleton of the story is real. The fabric or fill in part of the story is mostly fiction. The people and the names used in this book are not real; except where specifically stated. And that's made clear.

However, some of the things and events about the real characters are maybe, more or less, pleasantly creative. Some of the not real characters are loosely based upon people, who may have been real.

Most of the words, actions and thoughts given to the people are things that happened or could have happened or are just plain made up. They are things that could be possible, if not at times, too probable. The writer makes little or no distinction about anything in doubt. The reader assumes all responsibility in guessing which is which.

As regards to shared events and times, people who grew up with the writer will not remember the same things or they wouldn't tell the story this way. They would even say the writer didn't know what was going on. They would tell the story with a different flare or style. They would tell the real story. There would be as many real stories and ways to tell them, as there were individuals from that summer.

The use of vernacular language and slang, no matter how awkward or seemingly out of place, I feel is needed to convey things in the way they were really said and felt.

Do not look for a sense of immediacy in this story. There is no place to get to, "no bottom line." There is no great new, profound truth or concept to be unfolded before you. This is just a collection of snap shot memories that are twigs of fact and reality, woven (or twisted, if you prefer) around and embroidered within the writer's mind. These are snapshots of memories that invoked warm, appreciative feelings within the writer.

Most everyone has a baseball game, a trip to the farm, a picnic, a fishing trip, or person they remember from childhood. Maybe, one of these snap shots will remind you of that person or that event and your favorite summer.

So, this is going to be my story. And I truly hope you like it. This is what I remember and how much I loved hot dogs, hot tamales and bar-b-que cooked on number two wash tubs in the "Summer of '49."

# PART ONE

# THE PEOPLE AND THE TOWN

# WHAT?  THIS IS A STORY

## How It Started
## Present Day

"Chuck, can you make up another batch of margaritas? Oh where is he? I thought he was over by the door. Iola, have you got any more margaritas in the refrigerator?" called out Stella, one of the Saginaw transplants stopping by for a small get together.

"I don't think so Stella, but I'll have Charlie make another pitcher," replied Iola.

She insists upon calling me Charlie, and I didn't like that. I wanted to be and have been Chuck, every since I left my home town when I was 21.  But Iola won't let me get away with it because she always says my name is Charlie, and not Chuck.  At least you were Charlie in school and growing up in Saginaw.

"Iola was that Stella calling me?" I yelled to her out on the patio.

I was in the kitchen being creative preparing an Epicurean buffet along with regular tid-bits, done with a different flare and taste.  Iola would say I was making a mess.

We were entertaining old childhood friends, now retired, and living in hot and sunny Las Vegas. The guests, sipping margaritas and drinking beers, would rave about how everything tasted so good and tell me again that I should at least start a small catering business.

And once again, I would remind them of "Manuel Labor," a Mexican boy I grew up with and whom I didn't get along with at all.

And Iola would agree because she was always a step behind me, washing every spoon and knife, and any other item, the second I put it down. She felt I created a disaster area when and wherever I stopped to do something.

I felt that she over reacted and created a lot more work for both of us than necessary. Besides, I was going to clean up, as soon as I could get around to it.

Our home is near Sunrise Mountain, the extreme eastern side of the Las Vegas Valley. It was early evening. From the patio and pool area, the guests were enjoying the sight of the lights on the Strip and the rest of the valley coming to life.

The view pans from south, to the beginning of the Strip at Mandalay Bay, north to the end of the Strip at the Stratosphere. Then the lights of downtown Vegas merge with the Strip, and North Las Vegas and around to Nellis Air Force Base. Yes, it was, indeed, a very nice view.

At that moment, Eddie and Joyce, and her mother Mrs. Cooper, arrived. Mrs. Cooper and my mother were close friends, and Joyce got to play with a lot my sister's dolls, whenever she came over.

Yes, Mrs. Cooper knew me as Mickey since I was a rusty knee little boy. She knew all of us at the house and that we had all started out in one-room shacks in the country or beside some railroad track.

She looked at the front of the house and as she entered, she looked up at the high ceilings. She walked to the kitchen and family room and looked out at the patio and pool and the view of the Las Vegas valley.

She turned and said, "Mickey, this is a long way from Fifth and Farwell!"

"Yes ma'am," was all I could say.

Las Vegas and life today were really "a long way from Fifth and Farwell" in Saginaw, Michigan.

And that's what brings us to this point. These are snapshots of my memories about:

# SUMMER OF '49

## Hot Dogs, Hot Tamales, and Bar-b-que
## Cooked on Number Two Tubs

This collection of snapshots is seen through the eyes, confusion, wisdom, or something in between, of an 11-year-old boy, me. It is the views and memories of that boy who never seemed to be in step with kids or the grown up world around him.

Friends and others growing up with me will have a different story to tell. Other things will be of more importance to them. However, we all grew up in the same town, around the same time, and with pretty much the same ideas of what was right and what was wrong.

This is the time of my life, when I shed my snowsuit of the little boy and after the long winter of growing up, I can finally go out and play. It is the beginning of my dawning awareness of life around me.

This is when the mind begins to grow and send forth buds of awareness. Buds, like the spring crocuses that are the first of nature's flowery beauty, to pierce the frost of a long winter. Bright yellow petals, which forecast the promise of nature's colorful bounty of the summer that awaits us. This awakening takes place in a small, northern mid-western town called, Saginaw, Michigan.

Now older, and with my own grandchildren, I often sit alone or with childhood friends and wonder. We wonder how with nothing, we made a good life for ourselves and loved ones. We didn't know that we were poor or under privileged or that where we lived, the "first ward," was the ghetto. In terms of possession and status, everybody started out just about even.

We all marveled that almost all of the ones we grew up with had made it. Nothing was planned. Some had dreams and ambitions. But the only direction we were given, over and over again, was to "mount to somethin."

We had few black role models. There were two doctors, no teachers until the fifth grade, one lawyer and few or no other role models in our neighborhood. The only thing people kept telling us was, "'mount to somethin."

But it took everybody in town, watching out, caring enough and chastising (in those days that included whippings) when necessary, and just plain working together, that played a large role in keeping us straight. We all felt good and a comfortable warmth about our childhood years.

"Stay in school and go to college. Just don't work for GM. Stay out of those foundries if you can help it. Otherwise, get a job there and work hard and be proud 'cause it is honest work." That was our daily admonition or motto.

But college seemed like another world. It was hard to really understand what it was; let alone how to ever get there.

Many of our teachers, and other folks too, were saying "college for you would be a waste of time and money."

Those well-meaning people would advise us to "just stay out of trouble and get a good job in the foundry, marry and raise a good family. Be a credit to your race."

As I said, the boy telling this story was a Negro boy. The use of the term "black" and "African-American" were not acceptable to mainstream Negroes at that time. You see—they had just overcome being called colored.

Although the story is viewed through the eyes and filtered through the feelings of a black boy, it isn't just a black boy's story. Hopefully, you, the reader, can let these memories take you beyond that simplistic mind set. This is a family story. This is a small town, United States of America story...that is a still happening today story. This is a human story, which has pieces of all eleven-year-old boys, somewhere in it. And it happens in this boy's happy summer of '49.

Sure there was sadness and pain, and injustice in '49, just like at any other time. But this is meant to be a quietly happy, and kinda' easy going story about this boy's view of his hometown for just one brief period. A time that was a happy, carefree, fun-filled, idyllic and an all too short three months.

Now, right up front, it must be stated that although the story says it's about the summer of 1949, some things may creep in that, maybe didn't happen until '50 or '51, or maybe later. So let's not be a stickler for too much timing accuracy, or any other kind of accuracy.

And this story is about:
- Potter Street And People Watching On Hot Weekend Nights
- Saginaw, foundries, beans, and sugar beets.
- Fishing, a lot more than I ever wanted to do.
- Baseball, when it was the true number one sport in the nation.
- Friday night fish fries, and Saturday night rent parties and fried chicken and people having fun.
- A trip to a farm, yep, city kids on a real farm
- Waking up to a world outside of your home town, a trip down home
- Black Major League Baseball, the witnessing of the beginning of the death of a part of Americana
- Did we mention fishing
- Oh, and don't forget baseball

And then, there was eating. Eating all kinds of food. But the kids' favorite was eating lots and lots of hot dogs, hot tamales, pickled pig's feet, hog head cheese, pressed ham lunch meat, Valasic pickles (our home town pickle company), pickled ring bologna, fried fresh water pan fish and fried chicken. But the best eating was eating bar-b-que cooked on number two wash tubs.

# THE FAMILY

## Getting Ready to Go

"Mickey, come on! We're going to leave you. You'll have to walk. Then too, you'll have to buy your own ice cream. And you don't have any money, but I could loan you some, for a very small fee or Momma may not let you come at all."

"Nola Ruth, what is your brother doing?"

"I don't know Momma. I told him you said hurry up, but he won't answer me."

"Well, you tell him, he sure doesn't want me to come in there to get an answer out of him. So he'd better hurry, or we'll just go off and leave him, and he'll be stuck at home; and he won't be going anywhere, once we leave here. And tell him, 'don't even think about getting slick and slippin' out the back door because I'll have Miss Bernice and Miss Polly checkin' up on him.'"

"Lois, what is holding up that son of yours? I bet he wouldn't be so slow if he was going to "alum-a-ni field" to play baseball."

"Momma, you know as much as I do about what that boy is doing."

"All I know is he'd better come on or else we gonna' leave him."

"Well let's go Momma. He's had more than enough time to get ready. I'm tired of waiting and messing around on account of him, anyway."

"Let me go see what's holding that boy up. Mickey! What are you doing? Do you want me to come up there boy? You don't want your grandmother climbing those steps. I know you don't want that. Nola Ruth, go get in the car. If he ain't down in two shakes, we're gonna' leave his little, slow dusty butt."

"I'm comin' Grandma, right now. I couldn't find my other shoe."

"It's always some kind of excuse with you ain't it? Don't answer that, or we'll be here another ten minutes. Well, Lois, here's your son. Louis, you ready?"

"Yeah, I've been ready Momma."

"OK, let's go then."

"Get in the middle, Nola Ruth, you're the littlest."

"I was here first. You sit on the hump."

"But I'm the oldest so you have to sit in the middle."

"But I'm Momma, so I think this time Mickey you sit in the middle."

"Aw, mom, that ain't fair."

'You mean you're older than I am?"

"No."

"Then what's not fair about it, if the older one sets the rules?"

So there they go. The family: Grandma; Lois, the mother; Louis, Momma's friend; Nola Ruth, the seven year old sister; and Mickey, the eleven year old brother. And it is really his, or my story that's being told. So, it's time to tell you briefly, what this story is about.

## THE FAMILY

"Dough lord (meaning "oh lord"), dough lord. Y'all folks belong on 'telebision," Al, a friend of the family, used to look at our antics and say that.

And how right he was!

## Grandma

"What do you mean that pipe cost two-fifty? You're trying to get me riled up. Since when did you raise your prices? I can never trust you. I've always got to keep my eye on you," said Grandma.

*This is Grandma, the Head of the Family.*

*She was hard, loyal and trusting as far as she could throw you.*
*She was always looking for a new and easier way to make money.*
*She was our Father figure.*
*Mother at one time thought we loved her more,*
*that was never so, she was just more colorful.*

"Now Nola, you know, I always tell you the same price. You are the only one who always gives me trouble. You know I do not change my prices. You are just in one of your moods again and want to start trouble," said Mr. Johnson, the hardware store owner.

"What do you mean one of my moods again? You're the one starting trouble," said Grandma.

"I told you last week that you could not do it that way, particularly being a woman and all. Is just not the kind of job for a woman," said Mr. Johnson.

"Don't be tellin' me what's a woman's job. Nothin' ever get done waiting on you men. Ain't one in a bushel of ya', black or white, worth dependin' on," said Grandma.

Grandma was getting to the point where she was getting a little riled up. She was also beginning to feel a little put upon and put down by Mr. Johnson. He'd known her long enough to know not to tell her what a woman could and could not do. You didn't do that with Grandma. That was one sure way to get her mad.

But Mr. Johnson continued, "I told you I had a man that could do the job and get it passed inspection, something that you being a colored woman couldn't do on your own."

Mr. Johnson was about to enter a world where sight and sound are changed into strange things. He was about to enter Nola Hayes' "twilight zone."

Yep, Grandma, or Nola Hayes, also known as Mrs. Marshall, McFarland, Coleman, Mitchell, Queen Esther, or any name, which the exigencies of the moment might dictate, was a little four-foot ten dynamo of a hell-raising woman. She had been on her own since she was thirteen, and in her mind there was nothing she couldn't do.

Thus the quickest way to get her mad was to tell her "she couldn't do it; or that it was too big a job for her."

But if you really wanted to get her into turbo overdrive hot anger, tell her she couldn't do it "because she was a woman." That got her really red hot angry.

But for "sheer super anger" where she was beyond mad and unbridled fury kicked into gear, all you had to say was "a colored woman can't do it!" Then she would attack or go after you with the determination and tenacity of ten bulldogs going after one ham bone.

Those times, or now this time, was a time I really didn't like being around. Because she was about to tell that man, what she thought of his assessment of her capabilities. Mr. Johnson was about to become a "them."

At times like this when she got through telling "them" what they didn't know about what she could or could not do, whoever was unlucky enough to be "them" at that time; and at that spot, grandson, me, would feel very sorry for "them."

Grandma would tell "them" how this little black woman (oh, Grandma had no problems with using the term or word "black") could do anything she wanted to do, especially anything an old, white man (and it usually was a white store owner or business man) like you could do.

"Them" would want to hide or strangle that little woman.

Rainbows and rainbows of color her language could be. Marines, sailors, and construction workers discovered new colorful and juicy phrases to add to their lexicons.

But her language was not always colorful. Depending upon her surroundings (if other women, children, and people she didn't know were present), her language would be just lots and lots of various gray tones. Spoken in low and full volume ranges of sound and in pantomimes of a New York Jewish matron, or New Orleans French Quarter quadroons and mulattos.

Or she could just be a plain little black abused woman or a little Creole bayou girl, who may be down now, but one day, "I'm goin' to make it, no matter how you try to keep me down."

On these occasions the recipient of these words would have felt a whole lot better if Grandma had just given him a regular Nola Haye's cussing out.

It has been told and affirmed, that on some of these occasions, big burly white men's complexion would metamorphous from sickly "I need a tan" paisley white, skip past hot pink, and go instantaneously to crimson blood red.

Then came the high point in the setup of "them's."

Now restrained, heavy breathing, through flared nostrils could be observed.

And Grandma would look at "them" and say, "don't tell me you're thinking about hitting a little old lady, are you?"

At that point, everybody, within a hearing radius of thirteen and ½ feet, would stop whatever they were doing and look at that man, in such a way, that he would then turn a deep purple beet red and just clench his hands at his sides.  However, being a man, he would argue back a little but take the verbal lashing.

Then Grandma would turn, and with her head and nose held high say, "come on Mickey. I don't think we want to do business at this establishment."

Poor Mr. Johnson, all that abuse and no sale.  Grandma got some pipe from Kelly's store that he decided not to use.

Yes, Grandma, believed in a fair fight; even if you weren't fighting. She felt everything she did was fair.  She believed if a man was down, kick him.  If he survived it, she hadn't kicked him hard enough.  She didn't lose any fights that I know of.

## Grandma's Escorts

"Lois, did Mary pay her rent yet?" asked Grandma.

"No, Momma," said my Momma.

"That woman knows not to mess with my money.  Her rent is due at five o'clock on Friday, and she knows I don't play," grumbled Grandma.

"I 'specially don't need no stuff today cause I owe Cookie for that wall of hers he fixed last week," complained Grandma.

"And I done told her time and time again, her rent is due on Friday and not when she gets ready.  I'm gonna have to tell that heifer that if she can't do any better than this, I'm going to put her out.  I'm tired of her mess and her dirty little kids anyway," said Grandma.

"Are you through fixing dinner yet?"  Grandma asked Momma.

"No, not yet Momma.  It'll be a little while Momma," said Momma.

"Well I'm going to run down to the house and see what that woman is doing.  Come on Nola Ruth and walk with your Grandma," said Grandma.

So Grandma and Nola Ruth took off walking down to the apartment house, which was only a block away.  It was a slow and easy walk.  These were enjoyable and prideful walks for Grandma. She loved showing off her cute little granddaughter with the long wavy hair.

Grandma spoke to everybody, people sitting on the porch, working or playing in their yards on both sides of the street. She'd stop in the middle of the sidewalk and talk to other people who were passing by.

She stopped and talked to Jitterbug's grandmother. She waved and shouted something to Mr. Sam across the street at Kenny Holme's barber shop.

She just loved to talk. And Grandma could talk for days.

Some little boys waved at Nola Ruth and spoke politely to Grandma. They felt safe enough to be so daring because I was not around.

When they got to the apartment house, it was quiet, and they went around to the Norman street side and upstairs in the back.

Grandma called out, "Mary, Mary you home girl? How come you ain't sent the rent down?"

The door opened slightly, and Mary was holding on to it. You could tell that she been drinking little, well more than a little bit, she had been drinkin' a lot. And to top it off, she started off wrong.

"What cha' mean comin' up here old lady Hayes and demandin' somethin'. You ought to quit pestering people about that little bit of money. When I get around to it, I be down tomorrow. I will pay you when I pay you, if nothing comes up," slurred Mary.

"What do you mean, you will pay me when you'll pay me, and you'll pay me tomorrow, if nothing comes up?" said Grandma.

"You will pay me now or get your behind outta my house. Who you think you are telling me what you will do? I ain't one of those fools you been renting from before. Your rent is due at five o'clock on Friday, and I want my money or place empty and you out of it," Grandma shouted back.

"I don't know who you think you are, but you don't talk to me that way," said Mary

At that Mary opened the door wide or started to take a step toward Grandma. The poor thing, she was not aware of the fact that Grandma most always had a couple German escorts with her. They were a Mr. Smith and Mr. Wesson. Now everybody knew that she carried Mr. Smith and Wesson. Well if they didn't know, they suspected it and of course our two black vice cops knew.

And she was very fond of her escorts; therefore, she kept them close to her, in her bosom, and had developed a skill at calling upon them quickly when the need arose. In other words she had become a quick draw artist.

So before Mary could take one step the escorts were in hand and sight. But bad actin' Mary still was foolish enough to still try and take that first step.

Grandma's friends (both of them) immediately said hello to the ceiling over Mary's head. Mary for her part was not a very gracious hostess. She quickly jumped back into her apartment and slammed the door and started screaming.

Meanwhile, the little Mexican lady next door, who never got along with Grandma anyway, started chattering in Spanish and yelling at Grandma. She then ran into her house and called the police.

Grandma came down the stairs with little wide-eyed Nola Ruth stumbling in front of her. Grandma took her escorts and stuffed them down the front of Nola Ruth's panties and told Nola Ruth to walk carefully and take that package in her panties back home and give it to her mother.

Now this little seven year old girl knew absolutely nothing about guns and was not aware of the fact that Grandma had emptied it and put on the safety.

But Nola Ruth was afraid and scared out of her mind. There she was walking home with that object in front of her. She was afraid that it would go off and blow away what little bit of her there was, particularly that part of her she had come to know that was gonna be important one day.

She just wanted to get home as gently and as quickly as she could. However, all those people that Grandma had talked to wanted to talk to her now. Everybody in the neighborhood, friends, grown ups, even kids she didn't talk to, wanted to say hello and talk about nothing.

But she kept on walking and nodding. All she did was walk gingerly, taking little baby steps and nodding, afraid for her life.

Shortly the two vice squad cops, who Grandma knew, arrived on the scene. The Mexican lady ran over and in very broken English told the officers or tried to tell them what Grandma had done.

They went upstairs to talk to Mary, but by this time Mary had left. She was gone and was never really seen again. But the Mexican lady insisted on telling and retelling her story.

So the cops went through the motions of looking for bullet holes and said they couldn't find any. They told Grandma to go home and said to the Mexican lady that they would check back tomorrow with the woman in the apartment.

Then they turned and said, "Nola you still here? Go on home and quit giving us so much trouble."

A couple of hours later, after we were starting the Friday night fish fry party, the two vice squad cops dropped by to get a sandwich and to unofficially have a drink or two; officially they were still on duty. Then one of them handed Grandma a paper bag and said put something in this Nola and she did. It was a 38 Colt that had not been fired, not her escorts who were taking a shower by now.

There were no matching bullet holes in the apartment. The gun hadn't been fired. Mary didn't want to say nuthin'. Everybody was happy, except maybe Mary. We wondered, what ever happened to Mary? No we didn't.

Grandma never shot anyone, but she always said she would if someone insisted upon acting like a fool. At least I don't think she ever shot anyone

Bottom line: don't mess with Grandma's money.

With Grandma, you could make her mad real easy; and if she didn't whip you or punish you right then, she'd most likely forget about it. You could even get away with talking back a little if you weren't too close to her. She loved a good or even a bad argument. But you had better not roll your eyes. That would bring swift, painful, attention-getting retribution (I still don't know how you roll your eyes, but when someone does it to me, I know it).

She certainly believed in that bible saying about that not sparing the rod part. Grandma didn't stay mad for long, but she would talk about you forever. Sometimes you'd rather take the punishment, just to shut her up. But you didn't dare say it.

Yep, Grandma was the titular head of the family. To the outside world she ran everything, and what's more she even believed it. She was the front man for this mother and daughter show. In fact, she was a father figure.

Such was Grandma. A unique character, that we may tell more about in another story.

# Momma

Later Momma had to go to the hardware store.

"Hello Mr. Johnson. We need some pipe fittings and caulking. I understand that Momma was here last week. You two get into it again?" asked Momma.

"Now Lois, you know I try to get along with that woman and help whichever way I can, but your mother is impossible," said Mr. Johnson.

"You know how she is. She's forgotten about whatever she was arguing about the minute she walks out the door. And besides, you know you can't tell her it's not a woman's job," said Momma.

"I was just trying to help her get somebody that could do a real good job and at a cheap price," said Mr. Johnson.

"I'll talk to her about it. That's all I can do. You know she's not going to apologize," said Momma.

"If it wasn't for you Lois, I wouldn't have nothing to do with that woman. How can I help you?" asked Mr. Johnson.

Momma was again soothing hurt feeling. She always picked up the broken pieces and swept up the hurt feelings, after Grandma had ran through the crystal shop and stepped on toes and/or had kicked one or two people in the groin.

She was always busy taking care of the details, crossing "t's" and dotting "i's" and making sure the money was right.

Her job was to keep other people calm enough to let Grandma make them mad one more time. Momma was good at this. She knew how to get along with all kinds of people.

Although she had dropped out of school, she was smart and sharp at business. But she always doubted her gifts and was never comfortable with jumping to the head of anything. But others could see her smarts and were always volunteering her to head up, start up or straighten up something.

She later went back to school and graduated from high school. She went on and graduated from Cal State University, Northridge, with a bachelor's degree in education and received her state of California certification. She was very proud of that state certification, because she was fifty-six years old at the time.

Grandma talked the loudest and did all the yelling and raising sand. But Momma was the quiet one, the proper one. She spoke well and with proper diction and grammar, at all times, except in settings when it would be too much out of place. It was hard to make her mad. But when she got mad, look out. You would be better to jump off the Sixth Street bridge than to make Momma really mad.

As mother of Nola Ruth and I, she somehow managed to overcome her beginnings and proved to be the strongest one in the family. She was really the rock and the glue that held the family together.

Momma was a different kind of disciplinarian. She would give you rules and consequences. In gray areas she would give you a good length (not too long) of rope to hang yourself.

You did not want to make Momma mad.

You did not want to forget her birthday or mother's day.

You did not talk to back or look cross-eyed or roll your eyes at Momma

You did not want Momma to promise you punishment or a whippin'.

You did want stay on Momma's good side at all times

If you made Momma mad, your punishment was swift and/or preordained. If you forgot her birthday, for a month she would be ever so polite to you. But she would not talk to you, unless necessary. She forgot your school, church and other events until the last minute. She would make you walk to piano lessons. And you would have to get your own clothes together and hope that your pants had been washed. She would not play with you. You couldn't work on the big family puzzle, under the tablecloth on the dining room table. And worst of all, you got no hugs and kisses. The kids (well, it was me) only forgot one birthday.

If you talked back or looked funny to Momma, you got a stern look. And unlike kids of today, you didn't dare say, "what?" You knew what was what. And if you didn't, you acted like you did. And no matter whatever you were doing, that look was like a "cease and desist order" from the U. S. Supreme Court.

Now just in case the look didn't work, (I feel sorry for the young fool, usually Nola Ruth) Momma would start, not right away, a slow and casual stroll around. She would never miss a word in her conversation with the other adults. She would be just smiling and laughing and talking, as though nothing was on her mind or about to happen.

Now, this is the real painful and embarrassing part; every grown up around and half the other kids knew what was going to happen next. But would anyone warn the intended victim? No! The kids snickered while covering their mouths. The grown ups pretended that you were not even there. After all, these were the days when children were seen—if somebody wanted to—and not heard. And at moments like these, nobody saw the doomed child.

So now, Momma, having reached a spot in front of the condemned one, stands with her back to the one to be executed—and favoring more or less the victim's left side—delivers with flawless form, the old, forgotten, but ever so effective, "back-handed slap." A slap across the mouth, that should have never been talkin' in the first place. Momma didn't play. You just didn't talk back to, or act stupid with Momma.

If Momma promised you punishment, she delivered. She would say you are to get a whipping for that. And then she wouldn't do anything'. I would get an empty feeling in the pit of my stomach. I'd try to shake it off and go play and enjoy the day.

But every so often I'd look over my shoulder, straining to see her watching me from behind the mulberry trees, next to the Foleys, the Irish family next door.

Or she might be in the garden, pretending to pick some greens or carrots or radishes, while all the time watching my every move to see if I was going to add any more transgressions to her list.

Was that her among the peach trees? She knew that I knew, that she knew the peaches weren't ripe yet, and she knew that I knew she was watching me.

Oh, there she was in the back, at the side of the house, picking rhubarb. Was she gonna' make rhubarb pie? She knew how much I hated rhubarb. Was that going to be my punishment? No, I couldn't be so lucky and get off so easy.

I knew what she was like. She would wait until I was undressing to go to bed or when I was in bed and was just tumbling into dreamland, which took only two minutes in my case, and then rip off the covers and start whippin'.

She would be saying, "you thought I was kidding? Didn't you?"
"No ma'am"

"Oh yes you did. But I told you, you had to be punished, didn't I? And I couldn't go back on my word?"

"Yes ma'am, because I promise not to do that no more Momma, believe me."

"Oh, I do believe you sugar, but Momma can't go back on her word. That's the most important thing you can have —your word."

Oh, good sweet potatoes, I did not want to go through this all day; not this kind of torture. So I bolted to the house and ran up the front steps. There I found Momma, sitting on the porch with Grandma and our next door neighbor. She was the grandmother of a future hall of fame singer and composer, whom we may talk about in another story.

I couldn't hold it any longer and blurted out, "Momma can I please have my whippin' now, so I won't be worried about it all day?"

Everyone busted out laughing. "Lois, you done already give that boy a enuff of a whippin' for the whole afternoon. He don't need no mo," they said.

And Momma said, "since that's got you so worried I guess you've learned your lesson. Go on and play boy."

Such was Momma. She really was a unique character, whose life we may tell about in another story.

## Mr. Louis

"Louis, I said I want those green bags packed first," said Grandma.

"Momma, Lois said she doesn't want to take those green bags," said Mr. Louis.

"I'm tired of our gettin' in an argument between you and Lois about what I want done in my own house and car. I want my green bags," said Grandma.

"But they take up too much room. You know that and we got all the kids' stuff and our stuff," protested Mr. Louis.

Those kids can stay home for all I care. I need my green bags. Now put those bags in the car Louis," said Grandma .

As Mr. Louis' bad timing would have it, just as about the time that he had finished packing the green bags, Momma came out and asked,

"Louis, what are you doing with those? You know we don't have any room for those bags."

*Mr. Louis Ransom dressed up to go to a party in Fort Wayne, Indiana (I think).*

"Your mother insisted Lois. I told her what you said, but she wouldn't listen," said Mr. Louis.

"But when I tell you not to listen to her you know that if you ignore her she'll just fuss and walk away," said Momma.

"You know how your mother is when she gets upset and her mind made up. I get tired of arguing with her," said Mr. Louis.

"Well you know, you shouldn't have put those bags in the car because you know what problems that's going to cause. Now we gotta unpack the car. Why didn't you do it like I asked you to do?"

"I told you. I get tired of arguing with your mother. It's just easier to do what she says than to listen to her fuss. You go straighten out this with her," said Mr. Louis.

With that Momma bounded down the front steps, around the side of the house looking for grandma. She found her all right.

"Mother, Louis told you I said I didn't want those bags packed. They take up too much room, and the kids have to have some room;

otherwise, the trip is gonna be miserable." said Momma.

"Well, how am I going to take all my things? You never leave enough room for me," said Grandma.

"Well, you'll just have to do without this time and Louis told you I said not to pack those bags. Why didn't you check with me before you start changing things?" asked Momma.

It must be said at this point that Grandma was looking for a good or bad argument. She did not want to go on this trip, and she did not want to be bothered with the kids. So let us continue.

"And what Mr. So and So are you that I have to be checking with every minute, when I want something? You don't tell me what I can or can't do. You forgettin' yourself. I raised you heifer, so don't try and boss me now, cause you got a little education and think you know everything," said Grandma.

Momma side stepped the argument.

"Momma don't start no mess now. I ain't in the mood for it. So let's get packed and get out of here."

So there you have it. Mr. Louis, as usual, caught in the middle between Momma and grandma, about who said what, what to do and what not to do

Mr. Louis, Momma's friend of many years, was not strong enough to stand up to either Momma or particularly Grandma.

But Grandma was sometimes out and out mean; then Momma and she would clash. That usually didn't last long because by now Grandma had learned it was not in her best interest to make Momma too mad. And Mr. Louis knew that too.

The kids were friendly, happy, playful, and respectful, but could have shown him more love.

He played right field for the Saginaw Eagles. He was short and wiry and had compact arms solid, all muscle and strong. Of course, most of the men on our side of town were strong and solid, even if they weren't lean, especially those who worked for GM.

That meant working in the foundry at the roughest and hardest and dirtiest jobs. These were long before the days of full automation. The most common type of lift assist was an "arm-strong hoist." Your strong arms with one big heave-ho lift.

Yeah, Mr. Louis was tough. He didn't chastise the kids too much. I don't know if he ever said anything harsh to Nola Ruth. He was quiet but could hold his own with most anybody on Friday or Saturday night; except Momma or Grandma.

He worked all year at the foundry, and in the fall, for about two months, he'd work full time at the sugar beet refinery. That was a sixteen hour working day. It also meant we didn't have to buy any sugar for a year. Then at times he'd work at the gas station, at Washington and Tenth Streets.

But he got his greatest kick from playin' baseball. All spring and summer long there was two or three days of practice. Then on Sundays, it was the big game at Slick's Farm or the ride, with the family, up north to play teams from Midland or Coleman or somewhere.

He had an average bat, but he was tough on the bases. It was partly through him and Grandma's insatiable appetite for baseball that I became a little part, a very little part, of the last days of the Negro Major Leagues.

Nola Ruth and I can remember many fishing trips and ball games. I caught flyballs with Mr. Louis, and he showed me how to kill and clean chickens.

There were days that we went squirrel, and pheasant hunting. He spent a lot of good time with the kids, but when he and Momma broke up, there were no real tears or deep regrets. Through the years, the kids could have shown more love and less laughter.

Such was Mr. Louis. One day I will have to find more to tell about him.

## Nola Ruth

"Close your eyes and open your mouth, I won't do anything, I promise." I don't know how many times I pulled that trick on my sister. And of course, I always put something in her mouth. One day she caught on and has never believed another of my promises since.

Then I'd promise to give her a nickel if she didn't tell mom. So Momma would come home and ask if we had anything to tell. We would say no. I would not give Nola Ruth the nickel. She would run to tell Momma. Momma would not listen because Nola Ruth had missed her first shot and had lied and said everything was OK.

She was forever the brunt of my practical jokes Being my seven-year old kid sister was great fun and a great experience for her. For

*Nola Ruth, as kid sisters go, she was better than OK. She is about 9 years old here.*

example, she used to love being my jujitsu and judo partner.

In grade school she, could beat all the boys in her class. And those that were a year or two older she told them that her brother would beat them up. It was many years later when I learned why I got in so many fights and why so many of my sister's classmates acted strange around me.

In fact she became quite proficient in the art of self-defense. Something that a young bridegroom, who was six-foot two, discovered when he playfully pretended to throw a roundhouse right to the head of his four-foot, eleven ½ inch bride. She immediately had a post-traumatic flashback, and thought it was her brother, Mickey, pulling a sneak attack on her.

Nola Ruth, with the reflexes of a cat, blocked the threatening blow and went into a crouched position, twisting and turning in the direction the blow to allow the stronger opponent's weight and momentum to carry him forward and off balance. Then again with cat like nimbleness, she shifted her stance ever so slightly, and with one of her feet (I don't know which one) she came down hard on his arch and instep. And when he cried out in pain and reached to grab his foot, she presented him with a hard, correctly executed blow to the solar plexus. She caught herself at that instance, or else she may have never become the mother of his children.

Of course he wanted to know how badly Mickey had treated her as a child. He was assured that she gave as good as she got and more, because she always told Momma. Yes and how she told everything.

In fact she told everything all the time. Nola Ruth could not stop talking. If something was on her mind, it had to come out of her mouth. She was also very stubborn. She would not listen to advice, especially if it came from her brother. Time and again Momma would tell her to shut up or else get a whippin'. And she would turn and walk away with her face twisted into a dozen knots, and she knows how to twist a face.

Then less than seven and ½ minutes later, she would come back and say, "Momma, I know I'm goin' to get a whippin', but I just got to say this…"

And 43 and ½ times out of 45, she would get that whippin'.

Nola Ruth always had money to lend at rates that would make loan sharks drool; and I was always broke. Money just went. So in the end, Nola Ruth more than got even with that older brother of hers, me.

Such was Nola Ruth, and if I tell all those other stories that I may tell, you'll learn a lot more about her.

## Mickey, Charlie, Me

Now it's my turn. I'm Mickey, and eleven years old and just beginning to grasp the meaning of living in a world outside of my hometown. I'm opening my mind's eyes and seeing that the world is amazing, and I wanted to see it all.

Since this is my story, you the reader figure me out, because I ain't tellin'.

*Looking my best on Easter of 1953.*

## That's us

"Momma, Mickey's hiding the corner pieces of puzzle again. Like he always does, so that he can always put the last piece of the puzzle in. Momma tell him to put it back," said Nola Ruth.

"Mind your own business. I ain't doing no such thing Momma. Nola Ruth's just making that up," I said.

"Boy you'd better not be taking the pieces of that puzzle and hiding them," said Momma.

This was just another typical day in preparing for supper. Everyday, no matter how busy we were, no matter how many parties we gave, there was always the family meal.

The family was a small family business in a way. But everyday, even Fridays, when there were parties and socializing, after Mr. Louis got home from work, took a bath and got dressed, we would have dinner together.

Nola Ruth and I would set the dinner table. First, we would put newspapers over the family puzzle. Then we would put the oil tablecloth over the newspaper. Next came the cloth, tablecloth. Mother would make certain that we put the knives and forks, in the proper places—and turned the right way—with the water glasses in the right place. We would always forget the salt and pepper shakers. Many times we had to bring the saltbox to the table for Grandma, because there was never enough salt for her.

We would talk about things that happened during the day. The grown ups did most of the talking. We listened and learned things about various people throughout the city. We knew that if we ever repeated anything, it would mean our lives. We learned how to behave and how we were not to behave in certain situations. We were taught to always be proper and correct in public, particularly downtown and in the white world. We were taught to talk clearly and give full and complete answers. I regret that when I had a family, that my work, college, and life in general, did not allow me to do much of the same, with my children.

But that's the way it was in the summer of '49

I still remember.

# THE FRIENDS OF THE FAMILY

"If I still had a nickel for every nickel that I conned out of some fool that thought he was connin' me, I'd be a rich, little black woman right now. Fools think just because I'm a little bitty woman that they can run all over me," said Grandma.

"Yeah Mr. Clarence, she'd be a rich, little black woman now," said Nola Ruth.

She was walking behind them and repeating everything Grandma was saying.

"I told you I didn't want any of that junk in the house," said Grandma.

"She done told you she didn't like that junk Mr. Clarence," Nola Ruth paraphrased.

"If it ain't one thing, it's another with you," said Grandma. Of course, she used one or four or five colorful words.

"Yeah, it's always something with you," Nola Ruth was editing out the bad words as she echoed Grandma's words.

"I cain't get you to do anything right in the house," Grandma said rather loudly.

"And further more this is my house, and I'll put your little dusty butt out," Nola Ruth was now beginning to ad-lib from arguments in the past.

Momma immediately put her hand over Nola Ruth's mouth, grabbed her, and swung up away from Grandma.

The argument and sister's comments ended in one big belly laugh with that last ad-lib. Like I said, Nola Ruth from the day she could babble and talk was always running her mouth.

"Momma, you and Clarence cut that out now. Those fools in apartment number four moved out last night without telling anybody. Now we got things to do to get it ready to rent this weekend," said Momma.

Mr. Clarence and Grandma were into it again. Mr. Clarence was one of Grandma's holiday husbands. He lasted from one holiday almost to the next holiday.

"We've got to find Bob Scott and Cookie," said Momma.

"You know where we'll find Bob. He's at Claude's or Johnny William's Havana Gardens Beer Garden," said Grandma.

"We'll need Curly too, if he's in any kind of condition to work," said Momma.

Yes in order to keep things going, the old broken down apartment building and houses, plus the old cars, and the one half Way good house, we had to know a lot of "jack-leg" tradesmen, and some "jack of all trades." And some of them got to be good friends of the family.

After all, besides running rooming houses, we sold barbecue, gave rent parties and were active on many levels of the community. And there are a few other things that Grandma did that we won't tell about right now. That's for that other story, the writer, me, is going to write.

## Bob Scott

"Nola, have you been up to Quanicassee?" I hear they're catchin' perch up there as big as my hand, that's about as big as your arm," said Bob Scott.

"Naw, what're you doing tomorrow? We can run up there then and catch a mess of 'em," answered Grandma.

"I don't know yet. I'll have to give you a call sometime in the morning. I'll make it early. I like waking you up," replied Mr. Bob.

Now Bob Scott was a big burly broad barrel-chested man from Omaha, Nebraska. Mr. Bob was our electrician. Not only was he a good electrician. He was good at most handiwork type stuff around the house.

He was a true Midwestern plainsman that loved horses and the great outdoors. He was a man's man and spent all the time he could hunting, fishing, drinking hard, and when he had to, working hard.

He was about 6'-3" and every woman, well a lot of women, wanted him...and he knew it. He had broad, shoulders, a slim waist and narrow hips that didn't remain narrow as he got older. He had a light, reddish, skin complexion and had started to acquire a higher and higher forehead. His arms were like a weight lifter's. Mr. Bob was one of the most likable of all of Grandma's friends. He was loud and boisterous with the upbringing that could transform him into a gentleman, worthy of and able to grace any lady's parlor, or sit at any man's table. Mr. Bob was quite a character.

## Curly

Then there was Curly, the plumber. He was part Indian and had a reddish complexion and very soft curly hair. He couldn't read and write, but he knew plumbing. So if a city inspector knew Curly did the job, it had no trouble passing, even if he had covered it up or closed in the work. Curly was that good. He had a beautiful wife and good-looking children. He was a real nice guy, although I don't think I ever saw him refuse a drink.

## Cookie

Cookie was the family's carpenter. I really don't know too much about Cookie, except that he was always busy around the houses. Because he was one of Grandma's friends, he had to love fishing. I don't think he was too crazy about baseball. It seems as though all of Grandma's friends loved to fish and most loved to drink.

Running apartment houses and rooming houses meant that there were always a lot of damaged walls, windows and doors. In '49 you rented apartments and rooms by the week, not by a month. Momma and Grandma's rule was that your rent was due by five o'clock on

Friday. Not Saturday or Sunday and they were pretty strict about this. So when a family moved out on Friday, you had to have the place repaired, painted and ready to rent again by Monday. Most times when a family moved out, they were angry and left reminders of how they felt on the walls and doors.

For example, starting on Friday evening, someone would move out. All the family sprung in action, which included the kids. You had to check the premises, plumbing, the electrical, and find Bob Scott, Curly or Cookie.

Meanwhile, with ladders and scrapers, you start plastering, washing walls, and scrubbing floors and wood work. Then you'd paint the entire two, three, or four room apartment. By Saturday evening or Sunday afternoon, the apartment was being shown to new tenants.

The family turned the units around quickly. You couldn't make money on an empty apartment. And Momma and Grandma were about making money. Since we had an apartment in the back of our house and an apartment house down the street, Cookie was always busy.

Now of course, Momma and Grandma felt that the experiences of these professional tradesmen, the carpenter, the plumber, the electrician, would be wasted opportunities, if I did not work along side these men. So with my back (it was a gristle in those days, 'cause I was too young to have a back), skinny arms, and what little brains I possessed, they worked my tail off. So guess who vowed never to own apartment buildings when he was grown? That was stupid of him.

## Bee Catcher

"Hey, Bee catcher, where you going?" Grandma yelled across the street.

"I'm going over to the Fox Hole and play some 'coon-can'," he answered.

"Why don't you come on and take us up to Sebewaing? I want some rock bass and crappies too, if they're biting," yelled back Grandma.

"Well I don't know. I'm a little short, and I figured I could pick up a few bucks at Bum's place," he said.

"You ain't gonna do nothin' but loose the little money you got," laughed Grandma.

"Nola just because you beat somebody a few times, you think I cain't play?" Bee-Catcher shot back.

"Oh come on and let's go fishing man," said Grandma, not wanting to get in an argument now.

"Well OK. It's too early for the big money fish anyway."

So "a-fishin' they a-went" and guess who had to go with them, me.

Mr. Bee-Catcher was a general handyman and Grandma's special "catch all, she-can-get-him-to-do-anything helper." How he got that name is not known. There were no bees to catch around Saginaw. He was a medium-height, wiry man. He walked, kind of like leaning backwards, with a slow shuffling, slew-footed step, and he always had half a lip full of tobacco snuff. I think, he sort of liked Grandma. So that meant he had to love fishing. He also had to like a good ball game.

Now Bee Catcher didn't have a steady job. Therefore, Grandma always had him driving her somewhere. And he loved to go anywhere, especially somewhere.

When Grandma went fishin', a lot of times Momma had to stay at the house and take care of business or cleanup some thing Grandma had messed up. On those days, the kids would be Grandma's responsibility. And since Grandma was always messin' up or lookin' for a way to get away to go fishin', taking care of the kids got to be one of her main reasons to mess up a lot of things.

Grandma could never help out doing things because she had to take care of the kids. That's where Mickey learned to use the old, "I've got to study" trick to get out of house work.

Often when they went fishing, Bee Catcher and Grandma would leave out early in the morning, about five or six o'clock, and of course that meant the kids would have to get up early too.

Bee Catcher, would tie four or five- cane poles on top of that old 1936 Dodge sedan. It was mostly blue and was a car that had a lot of character. It also had rusty fenders, a hood that had to be tied down, and a lot of holes. But the best holes were the floor holes in the back seat. We would count the cracks in the pavement looking through those holes.

Bee Catcher, like Grandma, did not like to fish in boats. This meant that when you went fishing with them, you found some interesting places along the shore to fish. Sometimes it would be on logs sticking 10 ft. over the river. And other times, Bee Catcher would be perched precariously on top of rocks with a 5 feet drop to the river. But most of all, they liked fishing in different places. That meant they were always traveling all over the State of Michigan, looking for the next good spot to catch some crappies or rock bass. Mickey (me) was fished out for the next thirty-three and 1/3 years by the time I was thirteen.

Yes, Bee Catcher was a pretty good driver, and lots of fun to be around. He had a slow way of talkin' and with his slight southern accent, it took him 47 seconds to say, "Now  Nooo…llllllaaa."

But, in time, he developed one little problem. He reached the point where oncoming headlights bothered him a little bit. And he could not see well at night. Therefore he could not drive at night. It was his only problem. And since we were never out too late, because they had to get us home, Momma and Grandma put up with it.

But one night, on a twisting winding dirt road, things came to a head.

"What are you doing?" Momma and Grandma yelled.

"Well, ah, I can't see. The lights are blinding me," said the Bee Catcher.

"But there ain't no car lights, fool, that's only reflection off the trees," said Grandma.

He had opened the door and was trying to drive with the car door open, to keep from being blinded by the oncoming headlights. His reasoning sounded good except for the fact, there were no other cars on the road; therefore, no other headlights.

Up until this time, Momma had prided herself on not being able to drive. She had avoided a lot of things with Grandma, mainly fishing trips, and baseball games by not being able to drive. Of course, Grandma had always fussed at her about it.

"Well, I guess that does it! I'll have to learn to drive now," Momma said, while looking up at the sky through one of the car's roof holes.

So within two weeks, she passed her driving test and had her driving license. Now, Momma was stuck with driving Grandma to the hardware; to the house down the street; to Sanford Dam for fishing; to the courthouse for getting eviction notices and for anything else, Grandma could think of. Of course this meant that at other times, Momma could get away from Grandma by going to the lodge, the Girl Scout Brownie's meetings, church and the Elks club.

Although Bee Catcher still came around for odd jobs, we didn't see too much him any more. He had used up his usefulness to Grandma. She had a new pony to ride, namely Momma.

## Honey Dripper

Meet the Honey Dripper. Some say it was Honey DIPPER, like a popular song of the day. But I always called him Mr. Honey DRIPPER, and since I'm writing the story, it will be Mr. Honey Dripper.

Now Mr. Honey Dripper was the typical backyard garage mechanic. Every neighborhood and family had one, and he was ours. He could fix everybody's car, except his own.

He was a short little man with a receding hairline all the way back to his neck. He was also missing several front teeth. He was not a handsome man by any stretch of the imagination. Yet he had one of the prettiest wives, you'd ever want to see. He also had two very handsome sons. Nola Ruth and the boys played together frequently.

Nobody knows how Mr. Honey Dripper got his name, nor how he happened to marry such a pretty young girl. Nevertheless, Mrs. Honey Dripper was very much in love with that old, toothless man. Because many of Saginaw's fine, young Eagles tried to get her to fly away, but she stayed with her old man. And likewise, Mr. Honey Dripper loved his pretty little dove.

Honey Dripper's garage was located around the corner from grandma, so it was easy to get that old Dodge to him, even if it had to be pushed..

"Well Nola, what's the trouble this time?" the Dripper would ask, as he splayed a mouthful of spittle towards a spot where he thought nobody would step in it,

Mr. Honey Dripper was also a snuff dipper and always had a good-size plug stuck in his jaw. He and grandma got along great together because one was always trying to outdo the other. Grandma would catch him fixin' something that didn't need to be fixed. And he would catch grandma trying to pay him less than he thought he should get. And of course being a friend of grandma's, he had a love of fishing.

Honey Dripper really didn't have to create work on that Dodge, that car was on its last legs or wheels and should have been retired, long ago. Actually, it should have been scraped and burned, a long time ago. And grandma knew she was never going to pay Honey Dripper what he asked for. She would rather give anything other than money: fish, coon meat, venison, rabbits, even whiskey, but no money.

"I don't know what's wrong with it," said grandma. "You messed it up the last time you was working on it."

"You know I ain't messed up your car, Nola," said Honey Dripper.

"What then? Did you have one of yo' beer drunk buddies work it? I done told you, I don't want them working on my car. Anyway it ain't runnin' right, so fix it, like you was supposed to have done last time," said grandma in her normal voice, which meant that everybody in the garage heard her and were laughing at the usual greeting of these two old friends.

"Nola, I cain't get to your car until sometime tomorrow," said Honey Dripper.

"You got to get my car today, in about an hour. I got to get to Edenville. They are pulling out rock bass as big as bull dogs," said grandma.

"Woman, I told you I was backed up. I can't quit work on other people's cars to work on yours," said the Dripper.

I don't care what you do. I want my car in an hour Dusty Butt!" said grandma.

With that, she turned and walked away, and said, "I said make sure the car's ready."

Actually, it was done in about 45 minutes.

# A Special Memory

*A Special Tribute to Mr. Johnny and Miss Ophelia*
*Special Friends*

They were part of my village

There they were as I remembered them. They looked just the same as they did forty years ago. They were Mr. Johnny and Miss Ophelia. My fiancée and I were leaving the Big Boy's restaurant on Holland Street when I saw these two beautiful people. This couple had been friends of my mother during my childhood.

Mr. Johnny was a pitcher on our home team, the Saginaw Eagles, and Miss Ophelia was his wife. I grew up with their two sons. I was the team's batboy, and sometimes, Tyrone, the oldest son, would share the fun with me.

My mother and Miss Ophelia would sit in the stands together and take advantage of the setting to be a little less than ladylike; and yell their heads off at the players, umpires, other teams and fans. They had a good time together.

This couple was our friends. Not the closest of friends, but they were good friends and, on many occasions, we shared good times together.

The point that struck me that day, when seeing them after forty plus years, is the phrase that immediately came back to mind: "When you see one, you see the other."

My mother would say, "there goes Johnny and Ophelia. 'When you see one, you see the other.' They are always together. They're such a nice couple."

And they were both outwardly and from within. He was very handsome, and she was very beautiful. And they were very good and beautiful people, through and through.

It was just surprising that, that phrase came to mind and that it had stuck with me.

"When you see one, you see the other."

Those words were repeated many times while I was growing up. That's why, as a man in my fifties, to see Mr. Johnny and Miss Ophelia at breakfast together, was such a surprising and pleasant picture. Time had treated their looks kindly. To me, they hadn't changed at all.

And now here it was again, proof positive that, "When you see one, you see the other."

Seeing this couple, after so many years, added another thanks to the memories of my growing up years. Those beautiful people were part of the village that shaped and raised me. They didn't do anything that was spectacular; they were just there.

# THE FEEL AND ESSENCE
# OF POTTER STREET

## POTTER STREET
*(This is a song)*

Where were they going?
Potter Street!
*(make up your own music)*
"Hurry, hurry, hurry up, lets go."
"go where?"
"Potter Street"
"why?"
"stop askin' questions and lets go"
"what's the rush it ain't going nowhere?"
"boy, hurry up, hurry up and lets go!"
"We're goin' to Potter Street."
"why?"
    "because it's the everything street."
    "why, it's just another street."
    "it's the neat street. It's the street with the beat."
    "it's just the best happening street."
    "it's the come alive, magic street!"
    It's Potter Street

# This is Potter Street

Potter was a happy street, an everyday—the kids need some shoes street.

It was a "I missed her last Friday night" street.

It was a maybe "I can get lucky tonight" street.

It was a new dress for Nola Ruth, a cap gun for Mickey, and a new shirt for Mr. Louis street.

It was a "you can't go to the show unless you take your sister" street.

It was a get your chicken Saturday for Sunday chicken dinner street.

It was a VO premium blended whiskey, McNaughton's Canadian whiskey, and Champagne Velvet beer street

It was the cool, and so called half way nice, Elks Club street.

It was just so much more than our happenin' street.

It was a growin' up street.

It was a street where years later a gifted little boy played the harmonica for money in the hat.

The street meant more than just the stores, the picture show, the poultry market or RA's grocery store. It was more than the bars, cleaners, clubs and churches. It was like the main blood stream for our part of town.

Potter Street was magic!

During the week Potter was a business street.

There was Sun Down's market, to get the loaf of bread you needed.

The hardware store would cut that special length of pipe so you could get the water back on.

Momma could get her needles and sewing patterns at the dry goods store.

You could see a doctor.

You could get your medicine.

Everybody, at noon or at their lunch break, could fly into their favorite bar and find a hamburger, chili and a beer or two beers, or two shots and a beer waiting for them at their table.

Dads could stop and unwind at the bar before facing the kids and woman.

Commerce flourished across the street at the railroad. Starting early in the morning until late afternoon, trucks would arrive to load and unload big crates, stacks of little boxes, big and awkward looking pieces of machinery. There could be tillers for the farm or just big machines that you knew were going to a factory or the foundry.

There would be men with satchel bags buying tickets to go up north to sell high, or buy low, anything and everything.

## The Bricks and Stones - The Physical

The Potter Street, which you could see and walk, was not long, or wide or even grand—not even by Saginaw's standards. It was barely four or five blocks long. It was brick paved. And the bricks and car tires had a sometimes-rhythmic rumble, with a staccato of irregularly spaced, and just plain ordinary repair bumps, inserted by less than artistically gifted craftsmen. However, the overall effect on the car's passengers were that they received a free, total body massage treatment, that would cost them dearly today.

All the shops and stores were on the south side of the street. That was the only side of the street where you could walk comfortably. That was where the sidewalks were.

On the north side of the street there were no sidewalks. It was all Pere Marquette Railroad, tracks, truck-loading docks, and passenger and miscellaneous type ramps and steps.

On the other side of the street were all the stores and shops and so on. I don't remember them all but here is my best guess. Starting at Third Street just as you cross the tracks, there was an orange building, maybe it was a store. There was a small open lot and then Potter started right in front of our very own Dairy Queen. That's where I had my first hot fudge sundae, and I've been hooked every since. Next, we cross Third to the sidewalk side of Potter. You first pass RA's dad's market, where pretty little Jan worked. There were some other buildings and shops next to them.

Then there was the chicken market, or poultry market, if you want to be correct. Anyway, they sold forty-nine and ½ chickens for every one other kind of bird they sold. And a couple of years later, some of my buddies sold more chickens out the back door than the owner sold over the counter. As you may have noticed, no names were mentioned this time. Old friendship bonds, fear of lawsuits, and just plain knowing some of those young fools are now old and are still fools. And there ain't no telling what they still might do. So moving on. Next there was a cleaners and then an empty lot.

Then there was Oleanna's School of Cosmetology. It was a State of Michigan licensed beauty school. One of the real highlights of '49 was that Momma received her State of Michigan Cosmetology License. Everybody was very proud and pleased, and I felt a special pride because I had helped her study and learned quite a few things myself.

Now we come to one of the crowns of the street. The place that everybody went to. It was the State Movie Theater, or as we called it the Potter Street Show. And, if you were like me and had spent all your allowance, or didn't get any allowance and couldn't borrow or afford to borrow any money from your sister, then you hit the streets looking for pop and beer bottles.

In this arena the competition was tough. Every other guy in the neighborhood was doing the same thing. It only took six bottles to get the twelve cents admission, but you needed, if you could find enough bottles, to buy popcorn and an O'Henry candy bar. Most of the time, you did without the popcorn and settled for penny candy.

Then there was a hardware store, a bar, a restaurant, a shoe store, a dress shop, a church, a lot, a grocery store, a bar, a dry goods store, the Elks club and social lounge, Mr. Ellis's cleaners—whose one son became an All-American half back at Michigan State University. Then there was Doctor Cambridge's office building. As far as it was known, he was the town's first Negro doctor to build his own building.

And then going up and down the street were the street vendors. There was the peanut man, with hot roasted peanuts in the shell. The shells would make a mess all over the car, that the kids would have to clean up. But the peanuts were so good that it was worth it.

We also had the snow cone man, peddling his three wheeled cart. The cart contained a big block of ice, from which the snow cone artist would shave ice to make a perfect cone. Next he would carefully dribble your favorite flavor syrup, or mixture of syrups over the shaved ice. And then with chilled teeth, you'd start biting away at the cone.

This next gentleman was without doubt Saginaw's most important and famous street vendor. He was the "hot tamale man." He was without peer as regards to his product and remains so even until this day. Slowly he would drive up and down the street before heading up to Sixth St. or Gaines Barber Shop or over to the spots on Washington. But whereever he went, he'd always came back to Potter Street. People would be stopping him all night long, and he never ran out of tamales for too long. No weekend was complete without having one of his tamales.

Now just around the corner on Washington was the Mexican restaurant, where you got your tacos or other Mexican food.

Negroes and Mexicans lived together in Saginaw and ate a lot of the same foods. In fact, I was thirteen and ¾ years old before I learned there was a difference between soul food and Mexican food. This restaurant, while not located on Potter, was never the less part of the street

Now, I've probably missed more than a bar or two and a couple of stores; oh yes, an ice cream parlor. But you get the picture, that despite being such a short street, Potter, was nevertheless a busy, full of life street. Such was Potter Street.

But the railroad side of the street is where you saw the Potter Street that you felt. It was your best spot for people watchin'. That was the part of the real life of the street. You'd back the car up the docks or ramp, and you'd get a good view of the people side of the street, looking either way up and down the street.

You'd get there early, as soon as the loading docks closed, and the man of the house got home, bathed, shaved, and dressed. Of course there was always one slow poke in the group, who even though he'd had all day, was still the last to get ready. Once they got to Potter Street, the family would cruise slowly up and down those five blocks a couple of times, just to peruse the happenings. Now if it appeared that parking spaces were getting sparse, they'd find a spot and park right away. Then, they would cross the street and stroll up and down a few blocks.

## The Party Of Potter Street

### *The Magic Happens*

Getting Set –
But then comes the weekend. And Potter really came alive on Friday night. You know how that song goes, "the eagle flies on Friday,

and Saturday I go out to play."

Well in Saginaw, they didn't wait until Saturday to start playing. Friday night was the time "to let your hair down."  The time "to do your thing." Friday was "feel like cutting loose" time.

### *Early Friday Evening*

"Louis, are you going to find a place to park?"

"Yes Lois.  How is that spot?"

"That's OK."

So park we did. The kids, us, wanted something to eat right away. And as night follows day, we also wanted something to drink and something sweet.

"We only packed a sandwich apiece for you kids."

"Aw, mom."

"I made an extra one for you Mickey.  But when they're gone, that's it. We didn't come up here to be spending a whole lot of money."

So I would get by on two salami sandwiches, and sometimes Momma would slip in a peanut butter and jelly sandwich.  And me and Nola Ruth would wash it all down with some sweeter than sugar kool-aid.

The grown ups might have sandwiches or they'd have left-overs. They might buy something for themselves and share part of it with the kids.  If Momma was feeling good and had the time, she might cook some spaghetti or fry some fish, pork chops or chicken.  And if some tomatoes, carrots, or radishes from the garden were ripe or ready, she'd put those in a bag to take along to our Potter Street picnic.

After we were parked, we'd spread the old surplus army blankets on the car's hood, and laid out the food, the sandwiches, pork chops or chicken.  Sometimes it would be chunks of beer salami, pickled ring bologna, saltine crackers and some of that Pinconning cheese, they'd get on fishing trips. And we, the kids, had kool-aid, and in a bucket of ice in the back seat, was the beer or whisky for the grown-ups.

Momma or Grandma would give Nola Ruth and I our food.  And we with our food wrapped in brown paper or nothing at all, would lean, sit, or just plain hang out the back car windows eating while letting the people watching begin.

Our little eyes would open wide, to make sure they missed nothing. Look at all those people across the street and look how fine they're dressed. It was like being allowed to peek into the grown up world, without having to hide behind a closet door or under the porch, as was Nola Ruth's habit. We just couldn't wait to be grown. Oh, how beautiful it is to know so little about life and growing up at seven and eleven. Yes everything was so, so, so like magic.

# People Watching

### *The Little Big Boys*

It is now about 7:00 or so in the evening. Children are still out with their little friends. Some have been running up and down the street all day, buying ice cream, penny candy, snow cones, or begging the peanut man for just a few nuts, cause they didn't have any money.

"Ain't my fault. I got to make a living just like everybody else," he would say.

While at the same time wrapping up some nuts in a newspaper cone, and slipping them behind his back to the little sister, who sometimes really was surprised at the sly generosity of the peanut man with the rough hands.

Other kids are finally leaving out of the afternoon cowboy and cartoon matinee at the show. While others are starting to walk home. Their curfew will be comin' on, the streetlights. They have been window-shopping at the toys displayed next to dresses, shovels and pick axes in the stores all along the street.

"I'm gonna get me that fire engine, when I get enough money," "Fingers" would say.

"You ain't never gonna sell that many bottles," said Jugs.

"I ain't gonna be sellin' bottles forever, big head Jugs. I'm gonna get me a paper route. Then I'll make some real money," replied Fingers.

"Whose gonna give you a route?" said "Butter."

Paper routes were good jobs for kids. And to get one, somebody you knew and got along with, had to give you his route, when he got tired of it.

"Mickey!" said Fingers.

"Why's he gonna give you his route? He just got it last fall," said Jugs.

"His Grandma going down south this summer for about a month, and he wants to go," said Fingers.

"You mean he delivers papers all winter in the snow and cold and everything; now comes summer and he's gonna give it up? That's stupid," said Jugs.

"Naw, that's crazy, but you did say it was Mickey, didn't you?" said Butter.

"He ain't stupid, or crazy, just a little different," said Fingers.

Before he could finish, Butter, Jugs, and now Head, who had just joined the group, all yelled and pointedly corrected Fingers about Mickey, that he was crazy and stupid period.

"What do you mean a little different? He's crazy all the time and a whole lot different!" yelled the group.

"He ain't that different just because he's always into books and stuff, and goes to the museum and Hoyt Park," said Fingers.

"You mean you fell for that always carryin' a lot books routine of his? It's his front. He's fakin' it. His Grandma and Momma don't make him do so much housework if they think he's studying. As far as for going to all those places, his mother drags him along. He sure wouldn't go on his own. He ain't that smart, that would be sneaky, want to be cool, pencil-pointed, head boy," said Head.

"Head you're too hard on my man," the group says, while all the time holding their sides from laughing so hard.

"He does takes piano lessons from Mrs. Wickes. You know she's Sonny Stitt's, mother," said Fingers.

"Who is Sonny Stitt?" asked Beans, another addition to the group.

"What dummy? You don't know who Sonny Stitt is?" asked a surprised Fingers.

"Why he's the best musician and tenor sax player to come out of Saginaw, ever. out of Michigan, man. Where you been?" asked Jugs.

"Why he's been to Detroit, New York, and Europe and everywhere; that is everywhere Jazz is really understood," said Fingers.

"Shucks that ain't nothin'. Everybody that went to school with Sonny Stitt makes their kids take piano lessons from Mrs. Wickes," said Butter.

"You mean, his mother went to school with Sonny Stitt?" asked Jugs. "Man, I didn't know she was that old."

"Sonny Stitt ain't old, man. He's just hittin' his prime. He's considered one of the young horn blowers, just tearin' up in Detroit, making a name for himself. They want him back in New York too," said Butter.

"How come you know so much?" asked Fingers.

"I hear grown folks talkin' about him all the time, especially my Uncle James and some friends," replied Butter.

"I bet you do hear them talking, all right. Hidin' in your Momma's closet again, and listenin' to your uncle all right," said Head.

No sooner were the words out of his mouth, than Head, quickly spun and darted across the street, almost getting' hit by a car, before Butter could grab him or let him have one in that big fat mouth of his. Head just liked to always keep something stirred up, mostly people, and Butter was easy.

"Hey, did you hear that radio upstairs over RA's?" somebody asked.

"The Lone Ranger is coming on," someone else said.

"Yeah and the street lights are about to come on too. See you guys tomorrow," they all said.

With that, they took off running across the tracks and down the tracks.

Such was a typical Friday afternoon for the little, almost big boys.

### Their legacy to you or your "Brand" for life

There is one thing for sure; right or wrong, the group will figure you out—and their verdict will last your entire lifetime. No matter what you do later in life.

Dr. C. Browne, MD, is still Butter, the crybaby who tried to go with your sister.

Dr. W. Raymond, Ph.D., Ed., will forever be Fingers. Who you still have to watch very carefully and never let him get behind you.

Mr. W. Marshall, a national special insurance consultant, will always be Head. He can be and still is the worst signifier (one who makes crude, provocative and irritating comments about others) and bad mouthin', hurt your feeling, kind of talker, you'll never want to meet.  But he is still a true friend.

And even now, as granddads, when they get together, their wives say they revert to being grade schoolers.

One time, Mickey asked, "What was Jitterbug's real name?  I keep forgetting."

"Lunk," the worst signifier in the group said.  "Dang, I didn't know your name till you graduated.  You did graduate, didn't you?"

And all the other fellows started snickering and laughing' which in turn encourages Lunk or someone else.  And the game is on.

Everybody, for the rest of the time together, will be insulted completely and many times.  To join this group, you have to take a skin test, not for color—but to see how thick it is.

Oh, how the wives hate it when three or more fellows get together.  They act worse than kids and still lie and talk about each other, as though all those things happened the day before yesterday.

# HIGH SCHOOLERS - THE OLDER TEENS

*Have the girls home by 10:00*

## Bernie and Mary

Bernie and Mary were just turning the corner at 2nd St. heading for the show. Holding hands and smiling at each other, they were anxious to see the new movie and share some popcorn. Of course, they were also happy to be by themselves. Her baby brother would not be pestering them on the porch. And when she just happened to walk by his house, his little bratty sister wasn't broadcasting all over the street that, "Bernie's got a girl friend. Bernie's got a girl friend."

## The Ellis Boys

Running up the street were the Ellis boys, the two younger ones and Tank the older one. They wanted to get to the show and see what girls were out. Tank was a star football player. Several colleges and universities were interested in him.

He's the son, mentioned before, that went to Michigan State. Tank and the gang from Flint, Michigan, along with a host of guys from "the Valley," the "Saginaw Valley High School Conference," made

Michigan State a gridiron terror in those days. They kicked the University of Michigan's tail with regularity, after U of M was forced to play them, and also when State came into the Big Ten Conference.

With Tank along, the brothers were bound to have a good time. They were all good time and fun guys to be with. Plus, I'll never admit it, but it was said some girls thought they were cute. The younger brothers would rush up to the ticket window, and jostle, and fight over who was there first. They did it every week. Sometimes, the more sneaky and quiet one, Billy, would race ahead while Tank and Charles were talking to folks.

Nola Ruth and I laughed every time this comedy act was played. It was just another part of the big Potter Street picture show.

## Webbie and Art

Next came Webbie and a guy who looked like a Greek god, Art Lyles. There is no getting around it. The guy was just out and out Hollywood handsome. Anything of the female gender loved him. Young and old, black and white, puppy dogs, cats and kittens, and all varieties of women wanted a smile, and sometimes more, from this young copper tone teen. Despite all of this adulation, he handled it well and committed not more than his share of childhood screw ups.

I ran into him in 1956 in Newport, Rhode Island. I heard somebody yelling, "Mickey, Mickey." It had to be someone from Saginaw and someone, who had known me from grade school. I was a PFC in the U S Marine Corp. Reserve and a thousand miles from home. Who could be calling me, Mickey?

It was Art. What a surprise! Art was a Navy underwater demolition team member, one of the few blacks allowed in this elite Naval branch at that time. And he was married to Deedee, a beautiful girl, who was a grade ahead of me. She was indeed a beautiful girl.

Yep, Art would know me as Mickey. He and Webbie used to just love the job of baby sitting me. Actually my mother would ask Webbie's to watch me for a couple of hours.

But Miss Cora operated a beauty shop that was always busy, so guess who watched Mickey? It was Webbie and sometimes Art, who lived across the street.

Webbie was a star basketball player, who received a college

scholarship to attend Eastern Michigan College. He later played with the Harlem Globetrotters and the Harlem Magicians, but at 6'-0", or so, he never made it to the NBA. He also came along when there was a practice of having no more than two Negroes on a team.

Webbie and Art formed another nucleus of teenage interest on the street. But there was no competition between them, or with anybody, except the kids across the river at Arthur Hill High School. High school sports in small towns are an important part of its fabric and identity. It is today and was even more so in the summer of '49. Sports, for Negroes, especially then, gave them instant recognition and some opportunities. Webbie and Tank are still remembered and honored today, for what they were as sports figures then and for what they became as men.

## Back To The Street

At the show, other guys and girls would linger at the ticket window, while waiting to accidentally meet someone, that they were not really interested in.

And if that certain girl passed by, the so-called uninterested cool dude would say, "she's not my type."

And somebody like Bruno would say, "what, she ain't breathin'?"

And naturally, everybody laughed at Mr. Cool's expense.

Some of the teens would hang around the Dairy Queen, doing nothing special, just laughing and talking. A few more guys would go to the malt shop. And the real big spenders would buy their "friends," the girls not allowed to date yet, banana splits. You know that ice cream treat with three scopes of ice cream, cradled on a split banana, covered with whipped cream, with chocolate syrup poured over it. Then they'd sprinkle nuts and candy needles all over that. And to top it off, they'd add a big red cherry.

I loved cherries. I would eat them by the jar full. Momma gave up fighting it and started buying me little bottles of cherries from time to time.

The rest of the kids in the malt shop would collect pennies, to make nickels, to play the jukebox. It always had the latest records. They would dance a little, but no close up dancing in public.

A few kids hung out at some of the restaurants, but they didn't stay, once the grown ups started drifting in.  At this time of early evening, the street was slowly changing into an adults only world.

The teens ended up at the malt shop or at the dairy queen or just hanging out under a street light, clowning and singing.  This was the birth of "doo wop" and our version of "comedy night."

# The Movies

## Joe and Betty

"Joseph Gilmore, if you don't stop it, I ain't never going out with you again," said Betty.

"Shush, be quiet," came the reply from all those seated close by.

Obviously, some people wanted to watch the movie.  However, Joe was more interested in fooling with Betty than with watching the movie.

A few moments passed and Betty whispered, "OK, that's enough Joe; now quit.  You know how you get.  And I ain't gonna have my Momma lookin' at my clothes funny and askin' all kinds of questions.  Besides you know what my daddy would do to you, if he ever suspected that you even wanted to touch me."

"Aw, baby please.  I ain't doin' nothin'."

"I know you ain't because I'm leaving before they throw us out of here, with you actin' a fool and so on."

With that, Betty got up, and started stepping on toes and feet, trying to get by the folks on their row of seats.  The movie was almost over, and she'd all ready seen the end.  Now she could take her time walking home and listen to Joe lie and beg and act like she didn't know why he was walkin' behind her (that pun was definitely intended).

She wanted to leave?  That was great with him.  Joe was not the movie watchin' type.  He preferred live action thrillers; the kind of action where he usually got slapped.  And then, he'd walked behind the girl all the way home.

He would pretend to be apologizing and pleading and promising to behave himself next time, while all the time, saying to himself, that he loved the view from behind.  He really wasn't much for small talk only to the point of getting over; whatever that happened to be.

# Joyce and Marshall

Joyce and Marshall also were just leaving the movie. They had really watched the movie and liked it. And Marshall, being a nice guy, had only tried to touch Joyce once. And he drew back his hand, embarrassed that someone might have noticed when Joyce slapped it. After that, it took him all of ten minutes to ease his arm from the top of her seat to placing it on her shoulder. Once she had set the ground rules for the evening, they settled back, had two bags of popcorn, and enjoyed the movie. Why they even read all the actors' names at the end and tried to figure out which parts the bit actors played.

Leaving the show Joyce was giving Marshall that "I think you're nice" look. Once outside the show, the summer night was still warm. The sky was clear and the stars were bright; and a little sliver of moonlight put a nicely understated, finishing touch to the midnight blue sky. They both felt the beginning of teenage love. It was a tender love that never died.

"Marshall, can we share a strawberry malt?"

"Yeah, sure Joyce. Do you want to go the dairy queen or the malt shop?"

"Let's go to the malt shop. I've got a nickel for a record."

"That's all right. I'll play a record if you want."

So they started strolling up the street to the next block to the malt shop, holding hands and looking in the store windows along the way.

Nola Ruth thought they looked so cute together.

So like two comic book characters, Joyce and Marshall sat in a booth in the back. They shared one malt with two straws and grinning at each other, while listening to Johnny Ace on the juke box declaring "forever my darling, my love will be true. Always and forever, I'll love just you." It is nice to remember such young and innocent love.

Then Joyce noticed the time.

"We'd better hurry Marshall. My dad will get real mad, if I'm late—I'll be grounded."

So they hurried out of the malt shop, laughing and giggling at every thing and nothing. They were walking fast, skipping, and still holding hands. They hurried across the tracks and down Sears Street, to Eighth Street, and around the corner, a block, and across the street to her house. When they were on her porch, Marshall wanted to kiss her, and she wanted him to. But he didn't know how to go about it. He just held her hand and looked up and down at his feet and her eyes.

Finally he stammered, "I had a great time tonight. I hope we can do it again."

And Joyce, somewhat confused by his shyness said, "Sure, Marshall, I'd really like that."

With those words, she turned and opened the door to go in the house, and she froze. Daddy was standing there. Dad moved around her and called out to Marshall, before his foot could clear the bottom step.

"You got my daughter home late young man."

"Well sir, I was trying hard to get her back on time, sir. And so when I looked at my watch I thought we had made it, on time sir. I'm sorry sir."

"Well according to my watch, you're three and ½ minutes late. When I say 10:00 o'clock, boy, I mean 10 o'clock. Next time, you'd better check with my watch."

"Yes sir," answered a grateful Marshall.

Why was he grateful? Well Joyce's father said that there could be a next time. Now, if he could only get the courage and find the right time, to ask her out again. He never did find the right time.

## Bittersweet

It was indeed a love that lasted a lifetime. But, it was a love that was never fulfilled. Somehow, he could never find the right words, the right time, or the right place to tell her how much he cared.

She was so pretty and smart and bright, and out going, and popular. And everybody liked her. So many other guys were always talking to her. Marshall didn't think he had much of a chance. But he always thought she knew that he cared.

He always felt that, one day, after giving her a special smile, she would just know what he felt, and would return his smile. Anyway, after high school he joined the army, and soon he heard that Joyce had married someone else.

Joyce, for her part, never quite understood Marshall. She didn't know how shy he really was.

She didn't understand that every time he saw her, his broad smile and grin meant, "I'm crazy about you."

She completely missed a small compliment like, "you look nice today," which meant you look great every day.

She didn't know that he let Marvin get away with his corny jokes and debates about world peace or the junior choir, because he couldn't think of anything to talk about.

Joyce just thought that he really didn't think much about her. And besides Joyce was a busy, I mean, active, girl at school and church. So if you couldn't speak up, you got nowhere. That's true the world over; no matter what age you are.

But somehow, somewhere or some way, they did stumble, into the discovery of their long held and unspoken love. They didn't kiss or touch or say anything.

It happened years later when Marshall was on a business trip to town, and they were having lunch. While laughing at some joke or comment, they both turned their heads and their eyes; for the first time, they saw what each of them had been hiding. They discovered the depth of feelings that they had always shielded from each other.

They both felt an immediate flush and warmth and the exquisite, awareness of being in love. And just as their faces were about to flash into bright smiles and as a torrent of words was about gush forth, they froze. Because just as, quickly, in a blinding flash, they both felt the soul wrenching pain, of oh, no! Oh no, not now!

There was nothing they could do about this lost love, newly discovered. They could only continue to be old friends. They had to share, separately and silently, the martyrdom of self-sacrifice. Pain for a love lost is the most bittersweet pain, of all.

### Bittersweet

Bittersweet - because they had just been saved from never knowing.

Bittersweet - because now they knew why before, nothing else in their lives quite fit.

Bittersweet - because now that they had found the love they should have had, and it was too late.

Bittersweet - because they didn't know before how to show their real love.

Bittersweet - because there would always be a "but" if they tried to talked about it.

"But…"

If they had only known.

If he had only known to speak up.

If she had only known to trust her feelings.

If circumstance had not bound them to others.

If they weren't then so honorable.

But now years, children, first cars and first homes had passed them by. They had missed that part of life. Now, all they could be, were loving, loyal, devoted, close and warm friends.

" If…I"

" If…we"

" If…Life"

"And if love like this, was not so - so bittersweet."

## The Boys' Last Laugh

After the fellows had taken the girls home, they met up at "El Charos" Bar and Restaurant (Cabana). They would burst through the restaurant door and yell out, "give me a steak dinner." People would turn their heads and look at the uppity young uns' and wondered where they got that kind of money to be ordering steak, like they were some big time hustlers. How little those people knew.

A "steak dinner" was a plate of rice with a bean sauce. On top this you would carefully spoon all over it, an oily ground beef, tomato gravy that was hotter than anything in the world. You would then roll up a flour tortilla and eat and sweat, and eat and cry out that you were "mucho hombre" and continue to eat and sweat and love every mouthful.

Afterwards, the fellows would scatter to their separate homes. They'd start in the morning checking their traps, the fellows and the girls too to find the "happenin'" for Saturday night.

Such were high schoolers and their stars in the summer of '49

I still remember.

# The Magic Happens

## Potter Street Starts To Groove

Yeah, it was the time for the grown ups, the young ones, old ones, the single ones, the couples, the real nighthawks, and the hustlers. They really started hitting the street when the sun went down.

Some had to work Saturday and couldn't stay out too late; or hang too tough. But after the first show at the theater, it seemed like the street began to bulge at the seams with people. By now, almost all of the parking on both sides of the street was taken. The "beer gardens" were filling up. That's what bars used to be called.

Anyway, a funny thing about bar people is that those who sit at the bar will always sit at the bar, at every bar they go to, if they can. Table and booth sitters follow the same pattern, whatever, beer garden they go to. That was just an interesting observation. It doesn't really have anything to do with the story. It's just interesting.

The single women who just wanted to escape the kids or loneliness, in groups of two and three, would carefully venture forth. They were always being ever so mindful of protecting their reputations. Small towns could be cruel to a woman that crossed any line of proper conduct.

Single men, or those who acted single, would start just appearing; out of shadows, doorways, cars parked down the street, it seemed like from everywhere. They would drift in and out of the restaurants and bars with a smile on their lips and a searching look in their eyes.

Next, we'd see the couples, married or single, or those who were the same as married. And always there would be couples that shouldn't be couples, at least not in public. How they ever thought that they could play innocent or even sneak and hide, in a town where everybody knew everybody and everything about everybody, was being stupid.

## The Fallen Eagles

People began to intermingle—the young, the old, the seasoned vets, and the ones old enough to know better.

And it was always a special treat to spot the newly grown up ones try their wings and attempt to soar with the eagles of the street—only to crash and be picked over by the buzzards.

But once in a while a young eagle soared and sat with the other eagles and hawks, known as the real players. And wouldn't you know it, 7-1/2 times out 10, a lovely humming bird would dart out and pierce his inner ear. That young eagle would tumble into the cloudy abyss of family responsibility. Before he knew it, he would be pushing a baby carriage and walking proudly, with his shoulders thrown back just like all the other, young eagles. Yes "She" had clipped his wings, like Delia clipped Samson's hair. And that little humming bird had turned that young eagle into a proud young rooster.

And he was like all young fathers walking with their families on Friday, before the sun goes down. Because when the street lights come on, the strolling young families take the kids home and let them watch radio. All the other people and kids got into their cars and backed them up to the Pere Marquette railroad loading docks and waited for the real people party to begin.

When the sun gets low, the other people come out—the high school kids to catch the seven o'clock show at the Potter Street show and the real party people.

## Street People

Then came the nighthawks. The so-called real street people. They would strut up and down the street; looking for that fine someone or that exclusive happening that was too good for common folk; or that special somethin' to get into.

Some of the hawks would just lie back being too cool to be bothered. Later on that night, when it was nearing last call time at the beer gardens, and time to find out where the best after hours joint was that night, they'd be looking for just anyone or anything to bother.

Some couples stopped at the restaurant to get hamburgers, while waiting for the special Friday midnight show at the State Theater to start. This was the show the kids never got to see. Oh, how they couldn't wait to be grown.

There was Mr. Brainy Boy, in that brand new red Buick. Nola Ruth and I never did quite understand what he did for a living. He was always dressed up. He also seemed to have a lot of special lady friends. In fact, two of them were in the car with him now.

Oh, one of the ladies was Miss Irene. Nola Ruth and I called her, our favorite aunt. She was a nice person; although, Mr. Brainy Boy did not always treat her so nice. She would just smile then and said that, "he loved her more than the others." The family looked out for her. Grandma and her got along well. And she and Momma were friendly.

Going into the Elks was Saginaw's most debonair, Mr. Howard Heywood. He was always dressed like he had just stepped off a movie set with Denzel Washington. He was cool and clean. He knew how to charm everyone—men and women, young and old. And, whether by design or not, he had left miles of broken hearts behind him.

The Elks Club was of one the places to be. Howard walked in, smiled, and it was like the parting of the seas. Everyone turned, smiled, stepped aside, said hello, offered to buy him a drink. If some sweet things said their hello's too sweetly for the temperament and temper of her date, Howard would smile at such a guy; and if possible shake his hand, and say something like, "how's it going, my man. You're looking good tonight." And the way he said it and smiled, made even the most jealous guy smile embarrassingly. He indeed was quite a charmer.

Such was Howard in the summer of '49.

Such was the excitement of Potter Street in the summer of '49.

I still remember.

# THE CITY
# OVERVIEW OF THE TOWN

Saginaw was an old lumber town. At one time it was known as the lumber capital of the world. The town has also held the title "capital of the world" for foundries, gray iron foundries, malleable iron foundries, bean storage and shipping, and sugar beet refineries. It was indeed, a proud little city. In '49, it looked like Saginaw would grow and grow and become prosperous beyond anyone's dreams. Everybody felt that one day they could make it, what ever "make it" meant to them.

So, most of the people had a gritty determination and drive to get what they wanted. Now some people didn't want much or anything. Just like the poor, you will always have those people. But the feeling that sets the tone for this story is a happy, confident, outlook for the future. People believed that they could and would do something good with their life, and they did.

The geography of the city, East side and West side also reflected the eco-class status of the city. The east side was the "thems" that struggled to get anything and the few of them that thought they had it. The west side was "thoses" who thought they had most of it and had more to get. And the "thems" and "thoses" as in every story of small-town USA were separated by the railroad tracks or as in our town, the Saginaw River.

The river is one of the few rivers in the Western hemisphere that runs north (fear or research and work precludes me from being anymore definitive).  For many years it was the dump and junk yard for the gray-iron foundry, and all of the other industries and business located along it's banks.

The east side, my side of town, was also divided into the north side and south side.

And the Pere Marquette railroad tracks divided the city into the "First Ward" to the north, and south of the tracks was Potter Street and a narrow band of streets and blocks, known as "across the tracks." This geographical area was where most of the Negroes lived although there were significant numbers of people of color living on the south side.

I had lived on both the north and south side.  However, in '49, I was living on the north side and most of the story is about the north side.  That's the area of town where the good times were to be had. That's where Potter Street and all the other happening streets were located.

In our town, Negroes—the "well to do," poor, good, bad, the intelligent and not so smart—all lived in the same neighborhoods. Thus, everybody knew everyone or at least knew the families of everyone.  If a boy stopped over at a friend's house, and the grown ups didn't know him, they would immediately ask:

"Who's your people boy?"

And with the answer, the whole history of the boy would be revealed. What the family did for a living and its reputation.

It would be known that Jimmy, his oldest brother, was real bad and would end up in jail.  The grown ups would know that John, the boy's uncle, could not be trusted and had stolen some chickens from Miss Agnes out on 25th Street.

It was common knowledge that Mary, his older sister, was fast, and that Sadie, the oldest girl, was too scared to ever get married.  It would also be known that this boy was a good boy and looked like he was "goin' to 'mount" to something one day.

So you see, in a small city, living in a confined area, there was not too much that you could hide or that was not known about, "Yo' People."

My family, Momma and Grandma, knew everybody too (Nola Ruth knew 83-1/2 % of everybody. I knew almost nobody). The family had had rooming houses that provided rooms for many that were part of the great influx of foundry workers that came from the south. Most of them came during and right after World War II.

The foundries brought in a lot of men, and many came because a relative sent for them. It was not an easy transition to the northern foundries for some of these southern immigrants, especially, those not living with family or friends.

The foundries contracted with individual house owners to provide lodging for the new workers. There was no money paid to the owners. The foundries merely checked to see if there were a sufficient number of clean cots.

Thus sleeping space was at a premium. At the family's house, there were one or two double beds cots in each bedroom. And the men had to sleep by shifts. In other words, each bed was used by three men for eight hours each.

Our rooming houses were some of the cleanest in town, and the men in the house did not have that foundry odor filling the air. There were two pot belly stoves and a wood burning kitchen range. And on top of these stoves, there was a "number two wash tub" filled with hot water.

The rule of the house was that the very first thing you did after work was to get some hot water, fill a tub in the bathroom. Refill the tub on the stove and take a bath. Then you could go to sleep or sit in the living room or see if Grandma or Momma had cooked or would cook something. During the week this was not a good bet.

## Back To The City Geography

The other streets noted for fun and frolic were Washington and Sixth streets. On Sixth Street you start at the north end at Washington and travel to Norman Street, a distance of four blocks. Myrtle Street was a short block after Washington and ended at Sixth Street next was Farwell Street. We lived on Farwell, two houses on the other side of Fifth Street.

Then, came Dwight Street. Walt, one of toughest little guys in town, stayed on Dwight. Grown men didn't want to fight him. If you could hang with him, you'd better bring lunch and some left over supper. 'Cause the fight was not over till WG won. He was my buddy.

His older sister and Momma were close friends, and her oldest son was a handsome young man. He had the beauty and a fresh bright smile and the happy carefree expectancy of youth. He was 21 with lung cancer, and he had never smoked. His infectious smile and laughter was taken from us.

Norman Street was the boundary for the active tract of streets, Sixth Street. Washington Street, from Fourth Street north to Eighth Street also was an integral part of the fun times on Sixth Street. Together these streets were the "other side of the tracks" answer to Potter Street. But, Sixth Street was surrounded by neighborhoods and didn't have the variety of shops and stores like Potter. It was more residential. There were houses and homes between and surrounding the business stores. Sixth Street also had its picture show, the Gem Theater. There were also four pool halls, a cleaners, and a vacant lot or two, and the shoe shine stand.

But on the weekends, this "other side of the track's oasis" or "hole in the wall" held its own with the "across the tracks" Potter Street.

In the four blocks of Sixth, there were five grocery stores. Neil Johnson's was at Myrtle. Across the street, and half way between Myrtle and Farwell, was a Mexican store. Jerry's Market was at the corner of Farwell. That's where my family shopped.

Then, there was Sam Hall's Market, the biggest and only full service Negro owned market in town. Next, on the corner of Norman, there was Sam's, the Italian Market.

They all seemed to prosper. All the stores kept a weekly tab for their regular and mostly dependable customer's. The grocers would also let certain, kids take cigarettes and sometimes, even beer home if the parents called or sent a note.

Many years later, I went back to Jerry's Market to let Jerry know that, I in a small way, had made it in life. Of course, Jerry didn't remember me. There had been too many little boys, running in, out of breath, giving him a note, asking for a loaf of bread or a pack of cigarettes.

Anyhow, the neighborhood had changed. There were no more

peanut barrels by the door, nor jars of pickled pig knuckles and big sour pickles on the counter. The pickles were so big and fat that you had to bite into them at an angle with your body in a bent over position so to avoid the juice that would squirt from the first bite of the monster pickle.

There were no open counters without plexi-glass enclosures. Those clear plastic panels that are the sad sign of times now. Even Jerry had changed. He no longer had that easy smile at the corner of his lips. He looked like a harried, tired and somewhat, angry old man. He was constantly watching to catch which kid or wino would try to rip him off next. Jerry was just waiting for the time he could escape the confines of that store; that corner had changed, the Sixth and Farwell location. It was sad to see him that way. It was sadder to see the old streets.

## The Lord's Obstacle Course

The empty lot next to the shoe shine stand.

"Come on and help set up the chairs you guys. You never help do the hard work. You're always playing around with the wires and microphone and saying that that's all you can do. You know we don't have much time before we have to get started, so hurry up and 'plll..eeease' lend a hand for once." The preacher's girls were slightly irritated—all right, mad that the boys were not helping with the hard work.

The fellows replied that this (the microphones) was just as important as setting up the chairs.

"If people can't hear the preaching, all the chairs in the world ain't any good. And besides, you know how Daddy is about the microphones. We have to be able to cover the whole lot and across the street with the sound of his voice. He wants everyone to hear the message of the Lord."

Well once again it was late Saturday morning, and the children of the sanctified preacher were at the lot next to the shoe shine stand, getting ready for the outdoor fire and brimstone services that were held every Saturday afternoon during the summer months.

This was truly a family affair. The children and the mother and father made up a gospel band that played upbeat, bring your soul-to-Jesus music.

Many came to the lord at those gathering. The children in the band were very good. They all did very well in life.

As I remember (using my memory which by now you know is suspect or just plain bad) one brother played drum's, the other brother played trumpet, and one of the sisters played piano. The younger sister played the tambourine. Momma and Poppa and everybody else sang. On some Saturday afternoons, they sang so loud you could hear the music, blocks away. Understand, they had no high powered audio systems; so to hear the music blocks away, they had to play loud. They played a loud and upbeat gospel music. It was happy, and emotional music. It got into the crowd and moved them.

The people just passing by were an emotionally excited, curious and/or a captive crowd. Some would be walking by and before they knew it they were trapped and locked in a minimum security prison of their own making. They were confined to individual prison cells that were made of invisible walls of sin and regret. Some stayed and tried to get the message. Others stayed until the band stopped playing.

Then Rev. Beatty with his booming voice would give the people what they wanted to hear, a good blasting about sin; a denunciation of fornication and a hellfire preaching style.

He had stiff competition though, because he was located in the middle of the devil's playground. Next to his lot was the shoe shine stand with a jukebox and a gentleman, who knew how to sing the blues and a slow " I love you song."

And down the street was Johnny Williams' Havana Gardens Beer Garden. The only Negro owned bar in town.

And around the corner on Washington Street were Chet's and El Charo's Bar and Restaurant.

Across the street from the church lot was Sixth Street's newest addition to sin and frolic called the Las Vegas Bar, It was, otherwise, known as "the bucket of blood." Needless to say, the owner felt the name was not justified.

**It was not justified**
>   just because every weekend there was a cutting or two or three;
>   just because the bars' main clientele were Mexican workers;
>   just because they loved everybody else's women;
>   just because these men hated for anyone to talk to their women;

just because every weekend somebody did talk to their women;
just because they would get mad about this;
just because knives slashed the air and people too;
just because when opinions clash, the knives would flash.

And sometimes on the floor, along with broken bottles and glasses, there would be ears, fingers and broken teeth. But always without a doubt there would be enough blood to fill a bucket. However, the Las Vegas owner did not feel it right to call his place "the bucket of blood."

Thus, it was easy to see with these places, plus the pool halls and other activities on the street, how people got lost on the way to the church lot.

Some people said that even the lord would have trouble finding that lot on Sixth Street.

## Back To The Street

There was Kelly's Hardware and Dry Goods Store, a Lebanese owned store. Kelly had two sons, who from time to time, worked there. Neither of them liked to do it, but Pops ran a tight ship. That's why Kelly and Grandma got along so great. If any body could talk Kelly out of something, anything at all, Grandma was the one.

Red Tucker had one of the two drug stores on this, "the other side of the tracks." One of my best buddies worked there in later years. His best story was how one of our most upright church mothers dropped her bag and broke her bottle of rubbing alcohol.

She said, "Oh, my sonny, I broke my bottle of rubbing alcohol. Could you please give another one?"

Of course, every one else, in the drug store thought that the rubbing alcohol smelled like Gordon's Gin. But what did they know?

Oops, we missed the bookstore. It was located next to the shoe shine stand. Let's say this now. I was not always, as you see me now, a paragon of virtue and honesty. You see I always liked to read. And I read mostly non-fiction books, except when I went through the period when Mickey Splane's Mike Hammer, private-eye stories and Louis L'amour westerns had me hooked. Anyway, I would steal books from the rack in the back. I thought I had a fool proof set up.

If the owner caught me, I 'd tell the cops that the owner was illegally selling whiskey in the back room. Little did I know that the cops not only knew, but they were getting part of the profits and were some of the bookstore owner's best customers.

Anyway, the book store owner had already told Momma and Grandma about the pintsize crook. He had asked them not to say anything to me. I only swiped good books, not junk and trash like other kids. Oh, how dumb I was at 11years. Some of my acquaintances, like Lunk from those days, would say that I'm still that dumb. But what do they know?

On the corner of Dwight and Sixth, lived the pastor for the largest Baptist church in town, Mt. Olive. That was our family church. Almost everybody claimed some church as their home church, even if they didn't attend regularly or at all.

Across, the street from the church, at the corner of Norman Street and Sixth Street, was a big play field. The women's softball team practiced there, and they were very good. It was fast pitch softball. There was none of that slow pitch and blooper ball stuff. That was for little kids.

The women's team played in a league in which they had won the championship for a couple of years running. The teenage boys in the neighborhood often practiced with their team. Always thinking they could beat them. But the boys seldom won, and when they did, they would brag about it for weeks, while still losing everyday to the women. Getting used to hitting that fast pitch ball was difficult. The pitch would be on you before you knew it. You just learned to swing the instant the ball left the pitcher's hand.

The practices were almost as good as going to the game. There were spectators, kids riding bicycles, guys selling popcicles, and ice cream. You'd run across the street to Sam, the Italian's Market, and get a pop or penny candy. Or you could run across the street to Charlie's Jones house and get him to help make up a team to play the women.

Some guys from the Saginaw Eagles came to play the women sometimes. Mr. Eightball could not run and so he was always the coach. When he coached the boys, his signs were obvious because teenage boys didn't know too much about baseball signs and stuff.

So everybody was just out to have fun. And it was fun; people walking up and down the sidewalk, stopping, laughing and pointing. And just as the street lights came on, all the kids were gone.

The kids also played ball at the field. They could have three or four games going on at the same time. This was before the time when all kids' stuff and games had to be organized. They played for fun and the worst players were chosen last, but everybody played.

Sometimes there were thirteen guys in the field. And the girls played with the guys too, if they wanted to. It was no big deal. A lot of them were better than a lot of the fellows. The writer, me, was not normally chosen till near the end, unless LW and RG or a few more like them, were playing. Anyway, we just had fun until the streetlights came on, or from somebody's open window, the theme song for "Captain Midnight" was heard.

## The Free Picnic

"Come on Nola Ruth. They're gonna run out of candy bars if you don't come on," I was shouting upstairs to my sister. She could be so slow at times.

"I am coming, and if you keep yelling at me, I'm going to tell Grandma," Nola Ruth shouted back.

"Well you'd better tell on yourself too, cause you're louder than anybody," I shouted back.

"Grandma, Mickey's bothering me," yelled out the little story teller.

"I ain't doing nothing to her. She's taking all day to get ready so we can go," I said to Grandma, who was ignoring both of us.

"I'm ready," she said as she clomped down the stairs.

So off we were to the most "funnest" event of the summer. Yes, one of the most waited for and anticipated events of the year. It was the biggest fun on that lot, and it happened once every summer—the children's free picnic.

Kids waited for what seem like forever to find out when it was goin' to happen There were free hot dogs and pop, candy, Kool-Aid and potato chips and popcorn, corn on the cob, and whatever else was donated.

"Hey Lionel, let's get in the water balloon throwing contest," yelled Teddy from over by the ball field.

"You're supposed to toss it underhand dummy to keep from busting it," corrected Lionel.

"AW man quit being so technical, 'you wantta play or not," demanded Teddy.

"Sure let's go," said Lionel, feeling very good with himself that he got a rise out of Teddy.

So off they ran to the water balloon soaking contest.

"Look, wait up a minute," said Burny to Dan, two teen age boys. They were also on their way to the water balloon contest.

""They're about to start the girls' track races. I want to see this," said Burny.

"I hear that Frances and Ola are fast," said Burny.

"Yeah, me too," said Dan with a broad grin on face.

"Not like that, dummy. Your minds always in the gutter," said Burny as they ran to starting line.

"They do look cute, don't they?" said Dan as he turned and spoke to Shep. Burny was no fun.

"They are too young for you Dan. Man you need help," said Shep as he chuckled at Dan and just shook his head.

There were all kinds of games, like three legged races, water balloon fights, raw egg tossing, a track meet and of course, base ball, softball, dodge ball, volleyball, and there was boxing.

W. L. and I would box every year. After two rounds of punching (more like flailing) and too tired to lift our arms, the judges declared it a draw.

One of the big attractions was Superman. Superman, Mr. Watson, was Saginaw's hero. He played for the Saginaw Eagles and had a physique like a body builder. Every year he'd strip to his tee-shirt, and flex and show off his muscles. He would strut around lifting things and bending iron bars. The crowd would just be lovin' it up.

For his finale, he would position himself between the front ends of two cars, usually Fords. He would crouch low, hook his arm around the cars' front bumpers, and with great fanfare and straining, Superman would show that he was "the man." Superman would dramatically lift the front end and tires of those cars off the ground. Everybody cheered and whistled and shouted. They just loved it.

After the street lights came on, the little kids went home,

sometimes to return with their parents. Then that bar-b-que that had been cooking all day was brought out for the grown ups. Was it good? Of course it was. It was cooked on number two wash tubs, wasn't it?

Next, some of the local musicians would put on a jam session. And there would be jazz, blues, fun and love songs and dancing. It was the special event of the year for everybody.

Now, the free picnic, that is one memory that everybody remembers the same way. It was a happy day. Did I tell you that there were free hot dogs?

This picnic like every year was one of the highlights of the summer of '49.


Boy do I remember the hot dogs.

# THE WEEKEND

Yeah, blue collar, white collar and no collar. Saginaw was a working man's town. They worked five and six days a week. The foundries were for lunch pails and thermos bottles or greasy brown bags and fruit jars. It was sweat and hard work, foremen calling you names and you praying for quitting time Friday.

Friday was the beginning of the weekend and was the town's pressure release valve. It was the day for releasing of the tensions of the week. It was for throwing off the restraints that kept you tied up inside. It calmed the anger that wanted to rage against a name called or an insult suffered.

So Friday afternoon when the whistle blows:

Ezell rushes out of his jail of frustration;

Joe races home to his weekend of freedom.

Nate, says, "For two days I can live."

John takes a deep breath and lets out the anger for his name-calling foreman.

George let's out a gush of relief, and with a broad smile, brings a tired face back to life.

Al can rush to his favorite beer garden and clutch a cold Fox Deluxe.

Jimmy can have his double shot of Old Granddad.

So everybody lived for the weekend. That was the break that renewed your strength and will.

There were Friday night fish fries and card games. There were Saturday afternoon food sales, plates of bar-b-que, fish, chicken, and chitterlings for the church, the lodge, the majorettes; and when there was no other good cause, the family sold food.

There were Saturday evening rent parties with fried chicken, beer and drinks by the shot. And sometime Saturday night, somebody had to go up on Sixth Street or Potter Street and find the hot tamale man, Mr. Miller. It has been many, many years, and better hot tamales I have not found.

There was Sunday school and church on Sunday. And after church there was the movies or baseball.

But everything started on Friday at 3:00 when that foundry whistle blew. That whistle "got it on."

## Even the Music was Right on Time

"They call it stormy Monday, but Tuesday's just as bad,
Wednesday's worst and Thursday also sad
But the eagle flies on Friday......"
Then there's:
"Living for the weekend,"
"praying for the weekend,"
"begging for the weekend,"
"It's Friday, and it is the weekend."

Those are lines from songs old and somewhat new. But that's what you did if you were a working man in '49 in Saginaw. If you were a foundry worker or even if you were not, you still lived for the weekend.

Because come the week end
You paid the rent;
Tabs at the corner grocery store were supposed to be paid.
Al's loan was paid so you could borrow it back on Tuesday.
Loans from guys who weren't your friends were most definitely paid back.

The whole town got paid, movie shows, Granville's shoe store, and the downtown stores were alive with people buying. Red Tucker's drug store liked the weekend because folks would buy bottles and bottles of liquor. Mr. Tucker, did quite well on the weekend.

Yes, the whole town waited and lived for the working man's weekend. You see that "eagle" flew for just about everybody.

## Everybody Did the same
## Even the Ones Called "They"

The nameless "theys" did the same things as Ezell and the others. They hurried home and rushed to families.

They hurried to their favorite bar, sat back, and "cooled it."

They squeezed a nice cold bottle of beer with a whisky chaser.

They met their buddies and told jokes and lied 'bout everythin'.

And sometimes before going home, after being just about half-way high and feeling about, half-way-good, they wanted to act, 'bout, half-way foolish for 'bout half an hour.

They played their favorite songs on the jukebox.

They all started swaying to the blues.

They looked for a pretty face and a soft body to dance with and belly rolled and danced without moving their feet.

They all had German knackwurst, Mexican tacos or burritos, or soul fried fish and chicken

And always they stayed out later than they intended. But they didn't go home without some tacos from La Favorita, or hot tamales from the hot tamale man, or bar-b-que or fish dinners for the family.

But it was Friday, and you could sleep late Saturday. Your wife or woman will tell the kids to be quiet, and not to wake up daddy. And the kids will find somethin' to eat, go outside, and find some friends to play with.

So, sometimes Momma could slip back into bed with daddy. I guess she was tired and wanted some extra sleep too. There was and still is something special about Friday afternoon.

Now admittedly, some of the men stayed out most of or all night. Some of the single guys didn't have to do right. There was no home cooked meal waiting for them. All they'd do was cash their checks, go to a bar that they liked, and order one of those good home-cooked meals. They could get steak, pork chops, or any kind of meal they wanted. It didn't take much to get by as a single guy, if you had a job at the foundry.

Some of the real hard players would grab a little nap, because they intended to be out all night long. The "hard to the core" players, like the sporting life gents, didn't even need a nap and still stayed out all night long.

## Beer Gardens And The Blues

In the first ward,  the places that the everyday people went to were Chet's Beer Garden, the Wonder Bar, Johnny Williams' Beer Garden, and Charlie's Beer Garden.

Because, Saginaw is really an old German town, most of the bars were called "beer gardens." And beside the Mexican and Soul food, there was German snack food. Along with bags or bowls of peanuts, the beer gardens counter tops were crowded with jars of pickled pig knuckles, pickled pig ears, pickled eggs, pickled ring bologna, and big sour pickles, and sauerkraut and fat franks.

Grandma liked sauerkraut so much that she used to make it. I did not like it before '49, in '49, or any time since '49.

And in every beer garden, the jukeboxes would be going. Within that glass enclosure of multi-colored lights, you would hear Jimmy Reed, Muddy Waters, and John Lee Hooker.

There was Bull Moose Jackson. They say he had a big mouth, with "the voice" that caressed a woman like smooth velvet. There was handsome Larry Darnall, Lucky Millender, and the lithesome and winsome voice of Lil Green. There was the incomparable Mr. B, Billy Eckstine.

Then there was Arthur Prysock, Billie Holiday, and funnyman, saxman Louis Jordan, and the old black magic of Billy Daniels. We were moved by the sounds of the Mills Brothers, and what about, that little young singer by the name of Queen Esther Phillips. There was Johnny Hartman, Duke Ellington, Count Basie, Louis Armstrong, Ella Fitzgerald, Jimmy Witherspoon and Art Tatum.  The Ravens and the Ink Spots had bass singers who could really hit the low notes, and we all thought that we could go one note lower. All came alive for a nickel.

The list could go on and on , but the one type a song that was always heard. Especially as the night got older, was the latest or oldest of the blues. I did not understand it. People could be happy, and still they would want to hear the blues

As an 11 year old, I could never understand how people could love the blues, or even like that kind of music. The words just didn't make any sense.

She left you and you feel blue. You want to cry, but you're a man so you ain't gonna cry, but you feel some pain. You want her back. For what! (I didn't know much about girls. I was a little slow.)

Yo' woman's got a little upset because you stayed out late and spent a little money. But she don't have to get bent out all shape, over something like that.

And it don't be no good reason for her to take the kids and go back to her mother.

And what is this mess about another boyfriend, or man in her life? Why that's shameful. If she is gonna act crazy, then let her go, man.

Anyway the songs sounded sad and bad. There had to be a better way to express yourself than just listening to some slow dragging, music. And the songs were always sung by some guy you could barely understand, twanging away on a mouth organ and a one string guitar. It didn't sound like much of anything. and his voice was never a good singing voice. In fact, most of the voices were back aching, bad.

Yet people moved around in a trance or couples danced like they were lost in another world. Their eyes rolled up to the top of their heads, and they started shaking their heads, popping their fingers and saying, yeah, yeah yeah.

I never could understand why grown ups liked the blues, that is not until my girlfriend went out with my best friend and changed my life forever.

After that, I had my second girlfriend tell me she didn't want me "Nomo" (anymore). I was on a roll. It was the end. Then I began to understand the blues. I took classes given by Mr. Bobby Blue Bland.

And when my kids were growing up and I played the blues, and just like I used to look at my parents, they looked at me. It just proves that old saying the more things change, the more they stay the same.

Yes the music was rich and prolific and soulful. Full of throaty, gut wrenching pain or wild and crazy non-sense, like Cab Calloway's "Caldona, what makes yo' big head so hard?" There was sex and wild loving in some songs. But it was not described in detail, like songs of today. You had to use your imagination.

If you were a child, you didn't know what they were singing about, and thought that the music was either good or bad.

## Back To Friday Night

"No, no, you can't do it that way Nola. It won't work," said Mr. Bob.

"Yes, it will work, if you quit being so stubborn, and let a woman tell you, some thing, some time," replied Grandma.

And so it would go, back and forth, all day long.

"Ain't you got something else to do? Ain't you got to beat somebody else out of some money or check on something at one of your other shacks? Please leave, woman, so I can finish this job," he would beg.

"I'm going, and you'd better get it done right, or I'll come across them tracks, and drag you out of bed with that little skinny, yellow woman you got this week, and make you do it right," signified my Grandma.

"Woman, you'd better get outta' here before I forget that I'm a gentleman," bellowed Mr. Scott in mocked anger.

Grandma could make anyone get that way, upset that is.

Mr. Bob Scott did not work in the foundry. He was the electrician, you know, the one from Nebraska. But, never the less, he worked hard all week long. After all, he was just another working man.

He really worked hard, particularly if he had to do a job for Grandma that week.

He always wanted to do his work for the family in the first part of the week. He did not want Nola Hayes messin' up his weekends, which started at Claude's Beer Garden on Potter Street, if he was finishing or working on a job across the tracks. Later, he would move on down to the Elks Club. Then he would check out the Sportsman Club, which was all by itself on Kirk Street.

But his favorite bar as was Johnny Williams' Havana Gardens Beer Garden. Of course that did not stop him from keeping close tabs on what was happening at the other bars in town. Sometimes he would come by the house for a quick chicken or bar-b-que sandwich. Then he would continue on making his rounds of the beer gardens.

Later on, he would stop at Red Tucker's Drug Store for a fifth of V. O. or McNaughton's Canadian whiskey. Then he'd go across the street, Farwell, to go to Jerry's Market, where he would buy two or three beer jumbos.

I almost forgot about those jumbos. They were very popular. Mr. Bob could drink a jumbo by himself. Since then, I've learned that a lot of guys can do that.

Whatever time it was by then, he would find his way to our house. By this time he was hungry again and would come in the house, with his booming voice calling out, "What you got to eat in this shack, Nola? Lois will your momma let you fix up something for the old fool she works to death?"

"Lois, forget his yappin'. Tell him you'll fix him anything if he got some money," interrupted Grandma as if he wasn't in hearing distance.

"Money! How can I have any? You don't ever pay me. You get me up at all times of day and night, work me like a Mississippi field hand, and then don't want to have to pay me. Shoot woman as much work as I've done for you, you ought to feed me forever," boomed out his response.

"Ain't that much money in the world. Lois give that man somethin' so he can quit making me mess up my cards foolin' with him," said Grandma.

She was giving up the argument with Mr. Bob 'cause she was about to lose some money at coon-can.

Mr. Bob had a tremendous appetite, so whatever the main course was, he would take doubles on the meat, along with a generous serving of the side dishes. After eating and drinking half his jumbo, he and Grandma would always find something else to fuss about in a good-natured way.

His favorite expression was, "Nola, you don't know what you're talking about."

And Grandma would say, "you think you know everything. But you don't know nothing and you ain't nothing, but a big ignoramous."

Then they would play cards, together or against each other, all night long. I can't remember what Bob Scott's favorite card game was, but he played them all. He would lose a little money, win a little money, but when it was over, the only one that definitely made money was the house, and that was Grandma.

In writing these lines, I've discovered, that an 11-year-old can only look at the outside, and very little into the inside of the grown ups world. So what I just told you, doesn't tell you too much about the man, Mr. Bob. It didn't tell you about what he really felt. The only thing, I've told you, is he that he was a good man, and I liked him. He was one of the family's favorites, on Friday afternoon, on the weekend, on any day.

## Card Playing – Flies On My Wrist

By now, other friends were beginning to stop by. There was Mr. Bee Catcher, Mr. Curly, friends of Momma, and other friends of Grandma.

Mr. Bee Catcher came around because he loved to play "coon can." And he was quite good at it. It was a fast game, the way they played it. And it was cutthroat, down and dirty. It was no game for the weak. "Some cool cats can" and "some cool cats cain't." And if you cain't do, you'd better get out the way" is what the players said. It was many years before I learned to play the game, and Momma beat my socks off all the time. I'll never admit it, but my wife beats me most of the time too. I'm a much better gin rummy player.

But the meanest game of all was straight whist. It was vicious; straight up and down. There was no playing for the "kitty" and hoping that you guessed right. Trumps were known, and you had to play the cards as dealt just like life. There was supposed to be no talking and no signs or signals between partners. And if you wanted to keep a partner, the same partner or any partner, you'd better know how to play.

You have to keep your mind in the game; something, which I cannot do consistently. First, you have to remember what Trumps are. You must remember what card led. You must remember what suit that card was. You must remember who played the card. You must remember how many cards of that suit have been played, and it goes on and on. And I just can't stay tuned in for more than three or four hands. Therefore not many people will play with me—only my wife, sister or friends who play for fun and don't mind losing.

But if you played Momma, Grandma, or Aunt Lillian, you did not have to worry about remembering anything because they would remember everything for you. If you wanted to win it was best you did not let Momma and Grandma play together, or Mother and Aunt Lillian play together; because when they played together, the opposition's winning hopes and odds dropped dramatically. A few years later pinochle became their favorite game

"Rise and Fly" that's how the game was played. You had to win your hand, or rise up out of your chairs and fly away, or after the other team won five books. Of course the winning partners, and other observers would talk about how nice it was for the losers to warm the seats for the new real players. The losers would get constructive comments on how to become good at the game, or how to learn the game by playing someone they could beat, like their kids.

"Flies on my wrists, get away, get away. Flies on my wrists, you got to go, you got to go." I'll never forget Grandma saying that. Sitting down or standing up, shaking her hand, and saying, "flies on my wrists, they got to go, you got to go." And if you were those other players, it was your turn to rise and fly.

Or at another table you would hear the phrase, "we need new dolls, because these dolls can't dance." And that's how whist was played.

Sometimes Grandma would stand up, 'cause she'd say, "this hand is too good to sit down."

That expression lives on with her second great-granddaughter, Nola Ruth's daughter.

At another table somebody with tonk, five cards and under, can you beat that they yelled out.

Then there was someone saying, "you were standing pat with the wrong thing, cause I got pitty pat."

In the dining room they were playing po-keno, that's similar to bingo, and sharing the table with the sandwich eaters.

## F M FF- "Friday Means Fried Fish (or just food)

And all evening and night long, there were fried fresh water pan fish sandwiches and dinners.  We didn't fillet our pan fish and so they had a lot of bones, but we were used to them.  Some people liked their small fish fried hard so they didn't worry about the small bones.  I still like pan fish this way sometimes.

There were perch, crappies, rock bass, green bass, blue gills, sun fish, bull heads, willow cats, channel cats, carp, walleye pike, northern pike, large mouth bass small mouth bass, silver bass, and more.  The Michigan waters were bountiful.

Or it could be Saturday night and chicken, bar-b-que, fish, and anything else on hand was served.  It helped that we had a large kitchen.  Somebody could always help Momma with the cooking.

Other friends would drift in and out, throughout the evening.  Then, somebody, from another party that ran out of booze after 11 o'clock and Red Tucker's Drug Store was closed, would ask grandmother if she could help them out.  And frequently she could.  Or another party would run on a food, and this time, Momma helped them out.

## The Atmosphere Of The Setting

Friends playing cards, eating, laughing and listening to the music on our juke box.  The juke box was fascinating to me just watching the colored glass and colored lights, blink on and off, and marveling at the mechanical mechanisms taking the records from ordered slots and placing them on the turntable.  Then the arm of the phonograph comes over and gently lowers itself to start releasing the music and sounds, encoded in the little circular grooves running around those acetate discs.

People, friendly people, they were the only ones allowed in the family's home.  I became accustomed to having people around.  I did not interact with them.  I was just comfortable being an observer, watching the people live part of their weekend lives.

Peeking out from the edge of a window drape while out of sight and quiet, (but Momma was always aware of where I was), I would be  sitting on a little chair or cot tucked away in one of corners of the hexagon shaped alcove in the living room. Just observing the people. I don't know that I ever really learned anything though.

I still like having friendly people around. My wife and sister say that my parties are different because few of the people see or associate with each other, except at my parties. I'm accused of having a strange mix of friends. Be that as it may, I do like to entertain them by cooking big fancy meals or different combinations of meals.

## A Special Friday

When Aunt Lillian and Uncle Coy from Detroit, along with her brother Uncle Eugene stopped by, it was a special night. The piano

*Aunt Lillian and Momma.*
*A friendship closer and stronger than sisters.*

would-be rocking and rolling, because Uncle Eugene, played the piano.

Now he could not read music, not very well at least. And he had artificial legs, and when he played, the piano, he would pop his elbows. We used to love hearing him play, "Eugene's Boogie." That was a fast boogie woogie song, and with his artificial legs stomping the floor, along with his trick of popping his elbows, with his singing and our singing, we had great fun.

The jukebox went silent. Everybody was around the piano or

playing their favorite card game. Grandma and Mr. Bob were playing straight whist. Mr. Louis was playing tonk and Aunt Lillian was running back and forth helping Momma in the kitchen; although Momma told her to sit down and don't bother. Uncle Coy was in the corner, picking somebody's brain. He was always asking questions and reasons why of someone.

And Nola Ruth and I were just fascinated by Uncle Eugene and his piano playing. He would play well past our bedtime, and Momma didn't mind, and we didn't get sleepy. We just had more of a good time, when Uncle Eugene was playing the piano. It was just another added dimension to what was already a good night anyway.

Sometimes we ran out of prepared food. Then momma would fry some ham or bacon, eggs, grits, potatoes, or whatever. She would then whip up some biscuits that would melt in your mouth. My wife can make biscuits, that is, if she wanted to. She's only wanted to twice since we've been married, but that's another story

## The Party's Over

The juke box would come back on. "Stomping at the Savoy," and " One O'Clock Jump" would perk everybody up. But by this time the tune that really fit the goove was Erskine Hawkin's "After Hours." Then the Friday was over.

"The eagle flies on Friday and Saturday I did go out to play."

That's the way it was in the summer of '49.

I still remember.

# THE BAR-B-QUE

*Dorothy Mae, Momma, Nola Ruth, Me (Mickey)*
*Part of the Crew for any Barbeque Day.*
*Dorothy Mae, at about 3 years old, is a cousin of Stevie Wonder.*
*Taken in front of my home next door to Stevie's Grandparent's home*

Friday night balling and Saturday parties were an essential part of survival then. However, the survival food was the food from down home. And the gastronomical king each weekend was bar-b-que.

## The "Que"

May we now pause for a moment. Let's show proper reverence. We are now entering the artistic world of "Queing." (church choir music if you please).

Forget, just the weekend.

The epitome of good summertime living;

- the ritual that really made summer the bestest time of the year;
- the one thing everybody knew how to do better than any one else;
- was how to grill and eat those good, down home, tasting bar-b-que ribs.

I mean pure, unadulterated ribs with none of that sweet tasting, "Open-Pit" type sauce spread so thick that you can't really taste the meat. Yes, these ribs were pure and true to their origin and destiny in life. I mean, real down-home, cooked up north, spicy hot (if you like it) and tangy bar-b-que ribs that kept you biting your tongue and fingers and forever lickin' your lips. Ribs that were so good they made you try and eat your baby sister's.

Ribs that were slow cooked in the smoke of real wood charcoal; not fancy uniform briquettes. The smoke was a mesmerizing incense, of special clouds of joy. It was the kind of smoke that just got in your clothes and hung on.

The smoke that made everybody in the neighborhood, or people just passing by, turn and grin from ear to ear, and yell from across the street:

"Y'all better save some for me."

Little kids on their bikes would run into fences or trees because they were so wrapped up in watching the making of smoke and mouth watering, bar-b-que ribs.

### The Number Two Wash Tub

And those ribs were brought to the zenith of their perfection by being cooked, or grilled if you prefer, slowly, tenderly, lovingly and frequently basted on chicken wire fencing, strategically placed on the top of an old, highly decorated and well seasoned, number two wash tub.

In those days there were no fancy or plain grills that you purchased at K-Mart or Sears. There were no gourmet stainless steel, break the wallet and bank, showoff grills; instead, you used an old number two wash tub.

For those of you who don't know what a number two wash tub was or it might be (they are probably still being made today, somewhere); it is a galvanized steel or tin corrugated tub about three feet or so across and about a foot and one-half deep. When they're new, you use them for washing clothes and giving kids their Saturday night baths.

But when the tubs get old, they were not thrown away or relegated to a junkyard or a pristine landfill. No, the tub was about to become the most cherished possession of every household. It was to become a bar-b-que tub.

You will hear the refrains boldly shouted or quietly whispered, proclaiming;

"My Tub Cooks Better That Your Tub"
> my tub cooks better than yours
> my tub makes more bar-b-que than yours
> my tub makes a better charcoal fire than yours
> my tub's got more seasonin' than yours
> my tub's got the right number and positionin' of air holes
> my tub's just plain better than your tub.

Yes, possession of a good number two bar-b-que tub was a must for every house. However, every now and then the tub would "get lost or misplaced." And the whole household would be upset, especially Momma. Grandma would just be mad.

Grandma, would ask where was her bar-b-que tub? "You know the meat ain't gonna come out right on any other tub. Now, don't let me find out you kids been playin' with my tub and messed it up, cause if you have, ya'll is going to do some switch cutting today.

Now where's my tub?"

Of course we had been playing with it; but that's another story that we may get to.

To make a bar b-que tub, we'd take a pick or just an ax and punch half a dozen holes or so in the bottom and along side to christen the tub. Then you stacked up three or four house bricks or concrete blocks into three or four posts for tub support. Next, you'd scrounge up some chicken wire from somewhere; in those days it was everywhere.

Oh, chicken wire is a thin galvanized wire that's made up with a whole lot of hexagon shapes all twisted together, long ways and across ways. You could get it cut in almost any length you wanted. And it really was used to fence in chickens on a farm or in the city.

Now take about four or five house bricks and lay them flat in the bottom of the tub. You'd next take about three folds of chicken wire and set it on the bricks. This was the charcoal grate.

Now, you'd measure enough wire to over lap the top of tub and fold it over, again three or four times. You'd then mash it flat and that was your cooking grate.

Every now and then, we'd find a discarded ice box or refrigerator wire shelf and we used that along with the chicken wire. You now had all the grill you needed and the best grill, period!

At this point, all the skills required to make that one dollar, fifty cents, bar-b-que dinner , or that one dollar sandwich, came into play.

### *The Day Begins*

On bar-b-que day you'd wake up early, wash up, get dressed and go down to the front porch. You'd catch glimpses of the sun filtering through that big maple tree between your house and the McGees. You'd suck in a deep lung full of early morning, dew laden, fresh air. In '49 all houses had front porches and a good deal of your living was done on the front porch or in front of the house.

In the daytime kids played in the front of the house, and up and down the street. They were watched by all the grown ups. And in the evening, people sat on the porch and spoke to everyone who passed by. A lot of family living was geared to the front of the house. So come Friday or Saturday morning, it was natural to set up your "queing" in the front yard.

The first thing in the morning was to trim and season the meat. The next things in whatever order you got to them were start the fire and make the basting liquid. Start cooking the ribs. Make the sauce and boil it until it acquired that certain translucent gloss. Next make the cole slaw, green beans, and/or baked beans.

### The Fire

You'd start the fire with twisted newspaper pages, kindling (small, thin pieces of wood that catch fire quickly and last long enough to fire the charcoal), and real wood charcoal; without starter fluid, or match-light charcoal briquettes. Then add small pieces of charcoal and get a nice small bed of coals burning with a red glow underneath the bed. Now add more charcoal, being careful not smother the small bed of coals.

Once the coals had achieved a nice red glow, it was time for the "head what's in charge cook" to take over. After inspecting the fire, the cook added a few coals in this spot and that spot. Then using a sawed off broom handle or long stick, the coals would be moved to just the right spot to make sure the fire was spread evenly. After this ritual was completed and everything was all right, it was now time to bring on the meat.

### How Momma Did It

"Mickey you got to get up early tomorrow morning. So don't put in your mind to sleep late. I do not want any trouble getting you up. You know we've got to get this barbecue together for the Brownies. And you know what you've got to do. But I'll still have a list for you. Where are you? Where did you go? Did you hear me boy? I said I do not want you sleeping late tomorrow morning," called out Momma as I was trying to turn the corner at the staircase so I could've claimed not to have heard her. I was fast enough, but her voice was louder.

That meant a lot getting ready work had to be done. Before you just threw the meat on the cooking tubs, a lot of jobs had to be carried out in order to prepare that $1.50 dinner of cole slaw, baked beans or green beans, two slices of light or brown bread for the big end half slab of ribs, normally six bones. The small end dinner was $1.75.

In '49, ribs were not pre-packaged or/and trimmed neatly, like they are in the supermarkets of today. The spare ribs were just that, "spare ribs." Packing houses and big time super markets considered them a step above soup bones. Also, not everyone on the other side of town knew about bar-b-queing ribs.

The ribs were fatty and had large boned rib tip ends. The ribs were also from big hogs, with sometimes as many as sixteen bones per slab. So at home, the cook, or the cook's grunts, I mean, helpers, would trim off fat, cut off the rib tips and connecting back bones, and slit large bone ends, as required, to make for thorough cooking. This was hard work. From a large slab, you could easily trim off two pounds of fat and two or three pounds of rib tips and bones..

When the family "qued," on a sunny Saturday, they could easily sell up to one hundred dinners and sandwiches. That meant, there were a lot of ribs to trim. Even Mickey (that's me) trimmed ribs.

"Mickey . I want you to season the meat after we've finished the trimming. So get the salt and pepper, chili powder, paprika, cumin and lemon juice. And don't forget to peel enough garlic and onions. Now hurry up and get that done. I want the meat to set a little while before we get it on the fire. Then make up some basting water. You know, just some lemon juice and vinegar and water. You can add a little salt to it too," said Momma.

The basting sauce also was used to control fire flare ups.

The "bar-b-que" sauce is the mysterious elixir that makes ribs, "bar-b-que." Everybody has their own way of making it. The family had their recipe, and the proof that it was good are all the people who asked how the family made it or what was the recipe (that was a joke). And all those repeat buyers, who said, "I don't know what you put in that sauce but it "sho" is good. I'll take two dinners."

The sauce was made up in a big thirty-gallon pot. Grandma had gotten it from some place and had had it since she ran a boarding house at the Sault Ste. Marie in upper Michigan, in the late 20s.

The sauce ingredients were: water; vinegar; half a dozen or more of sliced lemons; lots of tomatoes-peeled, cored, diced; maybe a cup or so of catsup; a couple of cans of tomato sauce or paste; five or six sliced onions; maybe seven or eight, six or seven gloves of garlic; chili powder; salt, pepper, paprika, and half cup, maybe a whole cup of sugar, depending upon how much vinegar was used.

Now these were the ingredients. Don't be funny and try to be precise and ask for any measurement. The family, meaning Momma, didn't measure anything. They just knew when it tasted right.

Place the pot on stove; add water and other stuff when the cook said so. Bring it to a boil and simmer all day long or as long as the cook so orders. The cook was running this show, and everybody else was in the way if they didn't do what she said. "Nuff" said.

I helped do a lot of the preparation work and sometime I was allowed to hold the long fork and basting bottle and watch the ribs. I had made the mistake of starting to cook very at a very young age. I soloed in making his first cake at the age of nine.

However, my main job was to slice cabbage for cole slaw. Momma was very particular about her cole slaw. The cabbage was quartered and sliced very thinly. Noticed, the cabbage was " sliced very thinly," not chopped, not grated, but sliced very thinly. Also the onions were sliced very thin and so were the green peppers.

Then Momma took over. She added sweet relish, salad dressing, finely chopped garlic, salt and pepper, and sometimes grated carrots. Everything was added to taste. Momma seldom measured anything.

Since Saginaw was the world's bean capital in '49, making baked beans or anything else with beans was a no brainer. Momma's recipe used navy beans. The family's favorite beans, along with navy beans, were great northerns, small red kidneys, pintos, and butter beans.

But first, you had to pick the beans. The storage and processing methods were not very efficient in terms of separating beans and rocks and dirt.

After picking and washing the beans, the cooking started. The beans were first cooked with the basic items: salt, pepper, plenty of garlic, and several ham hocks and/or salt pork. This was done in another one of Grandma's big pots. Once the beans were done, they were transferred to a large blue porcelain roasting pan. The ham hocks were removed. Jowl bacon (made from the hog's jaw) and more salt pork were fried and added. Then came the tomato sauce, Ala-Ga syrup, molasses, chopped onions, and catsup. Bake in the oven for, however, long it took and again everybody wanted Momma's recipe.

Rib cooking started early in the morning. The tub could only hold two slabs and some ends and tips.  The family used two tubs.

Later they acquired a double wash tub and ringer tub, which meant that they increased production and improved on the cycle time. Therefore, with a minimal capital outlay, they were able to significantly increase total capacity and throughput throughout the entire production process and across all end product lines, with no appreciable increase in labor costs; thus realizing tremendous productivity gains, which, quite naturally, increased profits several fold.

In other words, when they scrounged up more tubs, they made a whole lot more money.

By this time, Grandma was dressed and was goin' up and down Sixth and Washington Streets, telling everyone that there was a barbecue sale—and they needed to come on by and buy 4 or 5 dinners. You can buy them for your kids, your wife, your girlfriend and her kids.  It's for a good cause.

If Grandma was one thing, she was a salesperson.  I believe she could sell anything to anybody, because she didn't take no for an answer.  You'd buy something from her, just to make her go away. She was that persistent, and believe me, she sold many barbecue dinners.

Meanwhile back at the house, the smell of barbecue was beginning to fill the neighborhood.  People would look out their windows and around the corner to see who was barbecueing.  And naturally they knew it was the family.  The only question was for whom were we barbecuing?  Was it for the club, the lodge, the church, the Brownies, or just for ourselves?  It really didn't matter, because they'd buy the barbecue anyway.

From everywhere they came to the barbecuing house.  They came and waited while the kids, who were playing in the yard next door, ran and fetched more paper plates, newspaper or pop, whenever a grown up wanted.  Hanging on and waiting, what seemed like forever, and yet they were "a keeping on comin' back" til they got their fill or there was "no mo'" bar-b-que.

It really was a bar-b-que fun time that summer of '49.

I still remember.

# GRASS CUTTING

Let's make this snap shot a Saturday when we are not barbecuing. It is one of those Saturday's that Mickey thinks he can sleep late; something that he does frequently when there is nothing that he wants to do. That doesn't mean that there aren't things to do. To be sure, there is always plenty to do. Since it is Saturday, Mickey's supposed to cut the grass. To say cut the grass was not fair because you did a whole lot more than just "cut the grass."

## *The House And Yard*

By this time in life, Grandma and Momma had purchased the old "Dooley" mansion, according to an old downtown banker, who had some grown up business with Grandma and Momma. It was a ten-room house, with a large upstairs playroom, that was eventually made into a three-room apartment. It was really just a big house, not a mansion.

The Dooleys had been a lumber baron family and had built this large house on a block of Farwell Street that had only three other houses on it—and they were all big houses.

One house was owned by the McGees, the grand parents of future, Hall of Fame singer and composer, Stevie Wonder. The other two houses were owned by the last Polish family in the area, the Foleys.

The Dooley house, (our house) had seen glorious days, when lumber was king and Saginaw was the lumber center of the world. Next to the house there was a large lot, that at one time, must have been the jeweled, garden envy of the neighborhood.

When the family bought the house, Momma made it her mission to restore the beauty of the yard. She remembered it when growing up. And since that was her mission, it also became Mickey's duty to see that her mission was carried out.

In the center of this big lot was a reflecting pool that was about ten feet in diameter. Around the front portion of the yard and on each end of the front porch were seven trellises of "seven sister climbing roses."

Along the south side of the lot was a row of about eight mulberry trees, all of different colored berries, ranging from white to pink, red, and deep purple. In the spring their blossoms were beautiful. It is only now while writing this, do I think of the real beauty of that yard. And how, after years of neglect, the family became the yard's new care givers.

Near the back of the lot, the family planted twenty three peach trees. The last forty feet of the lot was the family's vegetable garden. They grew a lot of just about everything. What they didn't eat right away, they either canned it or froze it. Nola Ruth still cans and freezes, even though her children are gone and it is now just her and James.

Along the side of the house, and between the side walkway, was a floral mixture of colorful bulb plants and perennials.

There were tulips, irisis, flags, and pretty orange poppies.

There were "sweet Williams" and lilies.

There were hollyhocks and sunflowers

There were those big bushes that had the pretty yellow blossoms every spring.

There were those big bushes that had the pretty white blossoms every spring.

There were the lilac bushes, white and lavender, with those beautiful blossoms and fragrance that is still so soft and mystifying.

There were pink and white rose bushes.

There were "American Beauty" rose bushes.

There were rhubarb and mint plants at the back of the walkway.

There were very thick, three and ½ foot high hedges across the front of the lot and house.

There were two flower beds of only tulips, behind the reflecting pool.

There were more flowers dotting the edges of the yard. They were mostly Irises, and another bulb plant that held its bloom all summer and had seed pods with little lavender flowers sticking out of the pods.

There were, of course, those first harbingers of the awakening of spring with those piercing little petals of sunshine yellow, the crocuses.

There were more types of flowers that came back every year, but memory fails me at the moment.

Yes, the Dooley house may have been a grand old house, but now it was just an old house, past it's glory days. It was just a big house, located in the wrong part of town.

### Cut the grass

"Mickey, get up and cut the grass, so we can go over to Marvin's house." yelled Freddy.

Freddy was and is a life long friend, that's so close we call each other cousin. He literally helped teach me how to walk. I get that story from Momma.

Now you see, just cutting the grass, that ain't true. Every weekend Momma and Grandma would say, "cut the grass." So I'd cut the grass and go play. But they would get mad. Why? Because they didn't say everything they meant and expected me to be able to read their minds and know that they meant more than just cut the grass. Of course I could only play this dumb once or twice. It didn't work the third time.

Cutting the grass meant;

- Cutting all the grass around the house and in the yard.
- Weeding the "morning glories, the "pansies" and all the flower beds.
- Weeding and cleaning underneath all the bushes and trees.
- Trimming all the climbing rose bushes and getting stuck and

pricked by thorns and the smaller rose bushes, and getting stuck and pricked by thorns.

- Cleaning and trimming all the big flowering bushes, the hedges.
- Clean up all the fallen mulberries so that they didn't draw flies.
- Then you had to rake up the grass clippings and other debris.
- And since it was forbidden and we dared it, grass did not grow between the sidewalk and the streets. Thus, to finish cutting the grass meant "sweeping the front yard." Such was life in the "First Ward."

So, don't you see? When they said cut the grass, no mention was made of all that other stuff you were supposed to do. It just wasn't fair.

There were no power mowers, weed wackers, electric grass edgers, electric hedge trimmers, or cute little electric chain saws for thick brush and dead tree limbs. These were the days of the fundamentalists, before the word had developed a religious connotation. All of those tools were fundamentally basic, or manual.

The grass mowers were reel type, push mowers; and pushing them was a real hard job. The mower always needed sharpening and the wheels always needed oiling. The wooden handles were always nicked and chipped, so you had to be careful not get splinters in your hands, or snag your clothes. Yes, cutting the grass was fundamentally a hard, back breaking Manual Labor job.

Grass trimming was done with hand held, grass scissors, that required you to get on your knees and meticulously cut each blade of grass individually. When I started naming the each separate clipping, I knew that I was near the edge; and I stepped back before total insanity engulfed me. Of course, some smart-alecky friends will contend even to this day that I missed that step and plunged over the edge—and have been crazy since then.

So you see, Saturday was the outside maintenance day. And to be honest, whether the family bar-b-qued or not, I still had to "cut the grass." Everything was done manually, and it is still too painful to describe how all of those other things made Saturday morning grass cutting, such cruel and unusually punishment, so we will just move on.

# The Saturday Breakfast

Before we could get started on such hard work, these growing boys and Mr. Louis needed grub, food, nourishment. We had to have a big breakfast.

Somewhere through the years or as they past, we lost the capacity to devour huge quantities of food (most of us). But there is still a restaurant called "Tony's" that still serves you a pound of bacon, a plate full of hash brown potatoes, 3 to 6 eggs, and all the coffee refills that you want as their standard breakfast. Up until the time I retired, I worked with a guy, who must have weighed all of one hundred and thirty pounds, who could consume one of those meals and still want three or four donuts. And he never gained a pound.

However, we started with three or four pounds of bacon, or jowl bacon that we cured, or salt pork, or real honest-to-goodness salt cured ham we cured ourselves, or smoke cured ham made by my dad.

But on Saturday morning, our favorite breakfast, was Momma's melt in your mouth pancakes. When she made pancakes, those things were big. Each pancake was the size of a dinner plate. And she had to cook at least 40 or 50 pancakes, if she, Grandma and Nola Ruth wanted anything to eat. Of course, if Uncle Coy or Aunt Lillian were staying over, all bets were off. Because by the time they got through talking, Mr. Bob, or someone else would stop by, and that meant at least another 15 or 20 pancakes.

Mr. Louis could eat 15 or so pancakes. I could eat at least a dozen or so; and Freddy was a light weight, he could only eat about 10 or so pancakes. And naturally, we had to wash it all down with glasses and glasses of milk.

Now one could get down to serious work and tackle the yard. After cutting the grass and cleaning the yard, Freddy and I asked Momma if she could take us to 23rd St. Otherwise, we'd have to ride our bicycles. Normally, Momma gave us a ride. Sometimes, my daddy came by and would give us a ride. Anyway, we ended up there somehow.

# 23rd Street

We were going to play with my cousins, Marvin and Ernestine, at Uncle Ernest and Aunt Flora's house.  Uncle Ernest was one of daddy's younger brothers.  In fact, he outlived all of his brothers. Marvin and I were the same age.  Ernestine , whom we called Stine, was three years younger than me, which made her one year older than Nola Ruth.

23rd St. was a country road, outside of the Saginaw city limits.  It was a narrow two lane dirt road with wide and deep ditches on each side of the road.  You were always afraid of running off the road and into one of those ditches, at least I was.  About a mile up the road you'd come to some railroad tracks.  And just across the tracks there was a road at a sharp right.  It carried you across the ditch on a shaky wooden bridge, that had no curbs or side rails.  This led you to Aunt Agnes' house.  She was not real a aunt, but a best friend of Freddy's mother.

Further down on 23rd St. you came to Aunt Cleo and Uncle Clyde's.  They too, were close friends of Freddy's mother.  Celo, also was the mother of my half-brother. Noah Henry Bruner.

Next door to Cleo and Clyde lived Old Lady Ewall.  Her name was one of the first names that I learned to say.  And of course, I said it with all the descriptive adjectives that Aunt Celo and Momma used when talking about old lady Ewall. And of course, those adjectives were not too flatteringly. After that, Momma and Celo learned to watch what they said around me; because at that age, I would tell everything I knew.

Even now, family and friends (both of them) still say that I tell everything I know.  Proof of that is that I'm writing this book, ain't I?

Further down the road was Uncle Albert's house.  He was daddy's youngest brother.

### *At Marvin's house*

Momma turned into the driveway and blew the car horn.  We all got out—Freddy, Nola Ruth and I, and Momma.  Nola Ruth, and I ran up the porch, and  Marvin and Ernestine met us at the door.  We all started laughing and shouting and talking at each other and ran out to the yard. Momma, Uncle Ernest, and Aunt Flora gossiped, I mean talked for a minute or two, and then Momma said that daddy would be back to pick us up later on, or that Mr. Louis would come back. Uncle Ernest said don't worry about it. He had come into the city, and he would drop us off at the house.

With that Momma left. Marvin, Freddy, and I took off to the fields. Uncle Ernest was still a farmer at heart and had planted corn, beans, other vegetables, and had quite a garden or small farm in the back.

There was a patch of woods, and we would always pretend we were in a deep wilderness, looking for bears and other wild animals. We had quite the imaginations. We did check on the fox traps, being careful to look out for injured foxes or coons. We would chase and scatter rabbits. Throw rocks at squirrels. And would always be momentarily scared when we flushed a quail or pheasants.

Farther back in the woods were creeks and big ponds. You would find mother ducks and their little ducklings learning the lessons of avoiding fools like us kids.

We would look for snakes, snails, worms and birds with broken wings—or ones that had fallen out of their nest. If we had our BB guns, we would shoot at squirrels on telephone poles or birds on telephone wires or rats in the field. And when we thought we were getting real good, we'd shoot at rabbits. We were not that good, too often. We'd mostly shoot at cans and bottles and twigs on trees, and argue about who was the best shot.

We looked for wild grapes or gooseberries and every now and then we come upon a mulberry tree and we saw crab apple trees everywhere. We'd sometimes find wild apple and pear trees. So we are always were eating something.

If we felt ambitious, we'd walk over to the muskrat farm. It was about a mile and half away.

Afterward we went back to house to get something to eat. Later we'd walk over to Uncle Albert's and play card games. We normally played "pitty-pat" and normally lost because I think Uncle Albert normally cheated. Anyway it was fun.

Next we'd walk down to see Aunt Cleo and Uncle Clyde. He was a slim, wiry-type guy, and he loved a farm too. We went there to get water from their pump. Their water seemed to taste the best or maybe it was just an excuse to go play in their water.

## For my Canadian Friends

Oh, I want to add this. Those ditches mentioned earlier taught us how to ice skate and play real hockey, ditch hockey. In the wintertime, the ditches filled with water would freeze harder than "John Henry's steel driving hammer." And we learned to play hockey the really rough way. Forget what those Canadians would say:

It's In The Ditches

It's in the ditches, where you really twisted knees, ankles, busted lips, and chipped teeth.

It's in the ditches where you developed skating power and finesse.

It's in the ditches where you had to jump over tree limb's, broken bottles, empty pork and beans cans.

It's in the ditches where you learned that sharp skates and strong ankles could cut through big and little twigs, laying twisted and frozen in the ice.

It's in the ditches where you mastered the art of jumping over some of those frozen twig half circles, embedded in the ice.

Thus to play hockey in the ditches was a real test of skill and guttiness.

Then there were the ice conditions. There were always rough spots in the ice. And the uneven spots of broken ice had rough spots. And that was the good ice.

Pushing that little puck around and putting it in the net was kids' stuff. We didn't play any of that, stopping play because the net got knocked out of position. We used a bushel basket that we froze in the ice, and our net wasn't goin' anywhere.

Yeah, the ditches. The ditches were the real challenge. The ditches, that's where real hockey was played. So put that in your "curling" rock, my crazy Canadian friends. That is if I have any left.

But all in all, when we went to 23rd Street, we didn't do anything that was exciting. We just had a lot of boys' fun.

And that's what we wanted to do, have fun in The Summer of '49.

I still remember.

# COLEMAN, MICHIGAN

"Next please, will the person next in line please step up," called out the clerk at the desk, who by this time was pretty tired. She had been on her feet all day and was ready to go home. The line had been long but was down to the last two or three people. Once again she called out, "next please."

"Hi, eh, hello I believe I'm next. I understand that you have applications for Seitner's Department store for female stock handlers?" Lillian asked.

"Name please, what is your name?" asked the tired clerk.

"My name is Lillian Sievers, spelled S-i-e-v-e-r-s," came the reply.

"Yes we do. The positions are for girls as after school work at several downtown department stores. Are you still in school?" asked the clerk.

"Yes, I am," came the reply.

"Well here is an application. Fill it out and take it to the store, and they will hire you." Stated the clerk.

"Thank you very much. Is that all there is?" asked Lillian.

"Yes all you need is an application from us," said the clerk.

"May I have an application for my friend also?" Lillian inquired.

"Where is your friend?" came the reply.

"She couldn't make it right now.  She had to help her mother," said Lillian.

"Well your friend will have to come down in person to get an application," Lillian was informed.

"Do you have many more applications left? inquired Lillian.

"Yes, we have several more left.  If your friend comes down today or tomorrow, there will be plenty left," assured the clerk.

"Thank you for the information.  I'll be sure she gets down here," answered Lillian.

About five or ten minutes later, in came an out of breath little thin or skinny girl.  There was no one in line and only the tired, sore foot clerk behind the counter.

"May I help you?" asked the clerk.

"Yes, ma'am," replied the neatly dressed teenager.  "I would like an application for after school work as a female stock handler in downtown department stores," requested the thin girl.

"We don't have any such applications," answered the clerk.

"But my friend said she got an application here," the girl gently protested.

"I don't know what you're talking about.  We don't do that type of work here," said our clerk.

With that the slight teenager left.  About twenty minutes passed and Lillian was standing in front of our tired clerk.

"You gave me these forms, didn't you?" asked Lillian.

"Yes the clerk," said after looking them over.

"And you told me that you had several more.  Do you still have them?" asked Lillian.

"Yes of course we do.  Just tell your friend to ask for me Peggy, and I'll see that she gets to work at the same store I sent you to," answered a willing and helpful Peggy.

"Oh, thank you, I told my friend you could help her.  Just a minute please," requested Lillian.

Out the door she went and in less than a minute, Lillian returned with her neatly dressed skinny friend.

"Oh Peggy, here's my friend.  She said you didn't know what she was talking about," said Lillian.

By this time several other staff members had gathered around, at a discreet distance of course, to witness the unfolding embarrassment.

"Didn't you just tell me that you didn't know anything about any job applications?" asked the thin one.

"Well, eh, you see, eh, actually well, you see, I eh, did not know that you meant those exact forms or applications," stammered a red faced Peggy.

This scenario was repeated many times as these two friends grew up. That slim girl was Momma and Lillian was her best friend.

Lillian was Canadian born and raised in Saginaw. She and mother became quite a pair. Aunt Lillian could easily pass for white, and Momma could easily pass for milk chocolate.

During the hard times of the thirties and forties, Aunt Lillian would go to a social or government agency and receive certain benefits or assistance. Momma would go in immediately after her, and she would be told that the agency didn't provide that benefit. Then Momma would say, but my friend just got some help. And again, the clerk or person would politely tell her that she was wrong. At this point, she would leave and, in less than two minutes, return with Aunt Lillian to reenact a scene like the one just described.

After the embarrassed and shocked clerks closed they're open mouths, Momma would get the same assistance that Aunt Lillian received.

They remained lifelong friends, and there was never anybody closer to either one of them, except each other.

When I was about six or seven, Miss Lillian and her husband Mr. Coy got tired of the Mr. and Miss titles. They demanded that since they knew us before we knew ourselves and had changed our diapers and baby sat us, they had clearly earned the right and respect of being, "AUNT LILLIAN and UNCLE COY." So they became aunt and uncle and the rest of her family became aunt, uncles and cousins.

Aunt Lillian had a sister who lived on a farm in Coleman, Michigan. On many weekends, Aunt Lillian and Uncle Coy stopped at our home on their way from Detroit, before going onto Coleman. Sometimes they would spend the night, and sometimes the next day, we would ride up to Coleman with them. So we got to know a little bit about the farm.

Nola Ruth and I were fascinated by the farm. We wanted to spend lots of time on the farm. So Aunt Lillian arranged a week long visit for us with her sister and her husband, Lester. However, Momma kept it a secret and didn't tell us. She waited until two days before we were to leave and said she had a surprise for us. After a day she told us we were going on a train trip. And that's all she said. No matter how much Nola Ruth begged (I was too old to beg like a girl) Momma wouldn't say anymore.

## The Day Of The Surprise

The sun is peeking around the edges of the window shade in my room, hoping to jar me awake with a golden ray by poking the closed and "don't-want-to-be -bothered' eyes of one lazy little boy. (I was not lazy, just efficient in my movements.) Ah ha, but the joke is on the sun this morning. This was a special morning, the Saturday morning, me and Nola Ruth had been waiting for what seemed like forever, but it had only been two days. We are going to take the train; take the train on a real train ride.

Then Momma said, "all right you children, hurry up, or we'll miss the train to Coleman."

And Coleman meant only one thing and that was we were going to the farm.

"Are we going to the farm Momma?" we asked.

"Yes!" she said.

So we were going all the way up to Coleman, Michigan, and stay at a farm, the Randall's farm. Where there were real live cows, hogs, chickens, and all kinds of animals. Why we were going to be a whole forty or fifty miles away.

Nola Ruth and I would also get to play with the Randall children. There was Delores, Ross, Lester, Marybelle and Joe. Only Delores and Ross could play all day. They were the young ones. The other ones had to work.

So it was off to the Pere Marquette Railroad Station. Nola Ruth and I quickey settled down by a window. Momma gave the tickets to the conductor, as the train began to leave the station.

It's funny but you don't notice it until you take a train ride. While riding, you see only the back side of the city, none of a city's best side. But once you get past the city and you are into the country, you see all the pretty green trees, pastures, farmhouses, and all that stuff that they put on postcards, and scenes like in Norman Rockwell's paintings.

The train wheels go click-a-tee-clack, making that sound as the rail cars wheels passes over the cracks in the rails. Most times, the "click-a-tee-clack" rhythm lulls you to sleep. Of course, normally, anything can put me to sleep, but not this time. I was too excited. It was a beautiful world out there, and I liked looking at the birch trees. The trees with the white bark that you could strip off in sheet-like pieces. The Indians would strip off the bark and make canoes. I was always gonna do that too. I never did. But it was fun reading about it in books at school.

Then there are all the pine trees, the beautiful evergreens, spruce and the Scotch pine. There was that blanket of pine needles on the ground, under the trees, making a soft, brown and beautiful crunchy and cushiony forest carpeting. I was just entranced by it all. It was a beautiful view of nature that I saw that day.

There were rivers and streams that ran along side the railroad tracks. On each little bridge that crossed the stream and in small boats dotting the rivers, people would be fishing. And between the tree branches, you'd catch glimpses of a fly fisherman casting for rainbow trout in a swift moving stream.

Then there was always the cabin far in the distance on a hill, rustic and with weather worn clapboards or logs, giving proud and silent testimony to its historical realness.

There were the swamps, now known as "wet lands" which always intruded when you least expected them.

It indeed was a fun train ride.

Now the tracks ended as far as we were concerned. We were in Coleman. The train ride was over. Now the real fun part was to begin.

## Greeting and Meeting

When we got off the train, we looked around for the Randalls, but we didn't see them. We, Nola Ruth and I, worried that they had gotten the days or time wrong? Or had something happened to them on the way to pick us up? We were like most kids overly anxious and bothersome.

Worrying and looking around, down the street, what we did see, made our eyes open wide.

"Horses! There, there, they've got horses! They're pulling a wagon with their horses," we shouted.

Yep, there was a hay-filled flatbed wagon being drawn by two horses, coming our way. And there was Ross and Delores, waving at us. Oh boy, our first treat in the country was gonna be a hay-ride.

Mr. Randall was playing his part to the hilt. He was dressed in his best farm bib overalls with a bright red flannel shirt, a wide brim straw hat, and a pair of black shiny cowboy boots. They all wore cowboy boots, because they did a lot of horse back riding. And to top off the picture, Mr. Randall, had a big yellow bandanna around his neck and a long straw, sticking from his mouth. Man, he was really living up the part.

"Well, howdy y'all. You folks looking for a ride? I'd be more than glad to help you out, if your goin' my way," said Mr. Randell, with a big grin that broke out into one big hearty laugh.

"Throw your stuff on the wagon and lets get goin'. We got 40 acres to plow 'a'for' noon, so we cain't be lolly gaggin'," said Mr. Randall, and try as he might, he couldn't keep a straight face as he said it.

"Hi Lois, you and the kids have a good trip? he asked.

So we piled all of our bags on the wagon, climbed on, laughing and giggling with Ross and Delores and started on the trip back to the farm in a real hay wagon. The trip was about 5 miles so it took a little while. Ross gave us some straw hats from his brother Joe. He knew that the sun would be hot and that it was a little bit of trip back to the house.

So as we traveled the country dirt roads, we saw rabbits, squirrels and lots of pine trees. There were wild grapevines hanging on trees and fences. There were some berries on trees that we were told not to eat because they're poisonous. And in rolling pastures we saw cows and horses and sheep.

We finally got to the farm, and turned off the road. We saw the farm house set back from the road, just like you see in the country magazines. There was a barn for cows and a pig-pen. There was a shop and shed for the farm equipment and tractor. There was a chicken coop and a vegetable garden next to the house. Although we had seen it before, it was like looking at it all for the first time.

Farther down the drive and past the barns were the fields where the crops were planted. Across the road was more pasture, and corn fields, otherwise known as the pheasant and deer storage field—I mean play field.

Nola Ruth and I immediately changed clothes. We were not dressed for the country. Afterwards, we went to see the barn. Meanwhile, Mrs. Randall had started making supper. And the grownups were having a lively, talking good time in the kitchen.

We ran after Ross and Delores as they raced toward the barn. Ross beat us all to the barn. Once inside the barn the city kids were awestruck. It was so big and open inside. There was hay piled here and there, and it seemed like everywhere. On one end, closed off from the rest of the barn, was the milking room. The cows were in little stalls. There were troughs at the cow's head and at its rear end. The function of each was obvious.

If you live in a city, you're used to the smell of all those good car exhaust fumes, and foundry smoke and odors. But when you go to the country, you get a whiff of real fresh air. And you know what? Fresh air smells funny.

Well on the farm, you get to smell fresh air and that ain't all. After a few moments in the barn, the city kids, us, were making faces and covering noses. We were now getting the real flavor of the barnyard and barn. We were really not aware that our sense of smell was so good, and that barn smells could be so penetrating. Ross and Delores laughed at us.

"You'll get used to it," they said.

I figured it must be an acquired sense of smell; one that I didn't think that I would acquire, but by the end of the week, we had.

Then, Ross, took us to where Joe and Lester Jr. were milking cows. Ross got under a cow, grabbed a cow tit, and squirted milk into his mouth. Wow, Nola Ruth and I had never seen that before, and we wanted to try it.

I jumped in the milking stall and grabbed the cow's tit, started to squeeze too. I squeezed one tit and then another. Nothing happened. The cow turned it's head and looked at me; and to this day, I believe the cow was laughing at me. Delores and everybody else laughed as I tried and tried to squeeze—and nothing came out.

Ross, said, "come on I'll show you how to do it later."

Meanwhile Delores was having a squeezing good time.

When you're on a farm, you have to careful where you walk. Outside there are all kinds of spots, piles, and patches you had better not step on. But in the barn, there is one particular area that you are supposed to be very careful around. That's the rear end of the cow stall or trough.

The next event to tell you about is kinda funny, but even after many years, a particular someone still doesn't think it's that funny.

Let me have someone else tell the story.

## Chucky Wachyostep

Hello, my name is Chucky Wachyostep, a private barn yard investigator. I'm a quiet guy who doesn't try to run your farm. I'm the one you call when there has been a big problem. The kind of problem, where you should have watched your step to avoid. The trouble is that I normally don't get called in on a case till it's too late for me to prevent the tragedy. When all they had to do was watch their step.

It had been a nice day; no mishaps. I was going to enjoy the setting sun, a good cold brewski and brats. Yep, I was gonna crank up the volume on that old Philco radio and listen to the Detroit Tigers pound some respect into the hated New York Yankees. But the phone rang.

The voice on the phone was shouting, and frantically shouting that I had to come. I could barely understand what he was saying, but I recognized the voice as being Les Randall. He had never called before so I knew he needed me. The brewski, the brats, and the ball game would have to wait. I had to see what was happening at Randall's Place.

I jumped into my pick up and tried to get her started. But she was actin' up again. So after a few choice greetings, she finally understood and started.

I tore out of the driveway onto a set of ruts that ran past my place and up to Lumberjack Jim's place. That's all it was; just two ruts that passed itself off as a road. It was potholed, dusty, winding and it was getting dark quick so my one headlight didn't help much. But I knew that road like the back of my hand, so I pushed on to see what was happening at the Randall Place.

I turned onto Les' road and spotted him at the front gate. He was waiting for me and pointed towards the barn. It was just as I had thought; the barn had claimed another victim. We got to the barn and there she was.

Barns can be treacherous. There are roosters that go wild, if you get too close to the hens. And sheep, who never heard of the lie that they were always docile and played follow the leader. Those soft, cuddly, woolly creatures can become vicious, head-butting ram rods (I don't know if I intended a pun or not)—and even those contented cows can deliver a kick that will send you into next week.

There are trap doors that send you tumbling down into nothing or on top of a wagon full of natural, unprocessed fertilizer (barn floor sweeping and animal excrement). Or stand in the wrong spot and grain, beans, or hay will rain down on a little body. Yes, a barn can be a war zone.

Oh, if they would just call me before it was too late, lives could be saved. Young minds could be forever spared, and battles with moods of insecurity and fits of insanity would be avoided. And otherwise, good and proud reputations would not forever be besmirched by one indiscreet moment of carelessness.

So you see, I'm dead serious when I tell you lives are irreparably changed because they don't call me before it happens. And cases like this one were particularly tragic because I could have saved this child.

It had happened in the early evening, when the cows had to come in. You know, you've got to unload them after a hard day of eating green grass and yellow hay and making it into white milk. (All right, so I'm not the first guy to tell you that joke. My Canadian friends still think it's funny). But unloaded or milked they had to be. Once again, it was one of those capers where they normally called me too late to save the victim.

I understand, that you might think that a trough would be easy to avoid. However, in a war zone the mine fields and anti-personnel mines are hidden. And in this case, the kind that I see much too often, the mines were intermittently covered by thin plank or innocent looking straw and hay.

So if you are not real careful or know your way around the barn, then tragedy would strike quickly; and afterwards, you'd call me, always too late. And on this day, tragedy struck.

There was only one belated warning, "Nola Ruth, be careful back there. Look out for that trough. 'Wat-ch-yo'-step," cried out Lester Jr.

But it was too little, and too late. Yep, you guessed it. Nola Ruth, not only stepped in it, but all of that little seven-year-old body fell into the cow's rear end trough. Everyone around sprang to her rescue.

And then they called me, "Chucky 'Watchyostep." I immediately set up a crisis intervention center and procedures and started grief counseling sessions (oh, I'm sorry, none of that kind of psychological crutch stuff or mind mumbo-jumbo soothing junk existed in those days). The only thing I could do was tell them how to clean up the situation. So I really didn't do anything. I'll let Mickey finish telling you this story.

That evening, Momma, had to strip off all of Nola Ruth's clothes and outside, on the pump pad, had to wash her off. Nola Ruth had long hair then, well past her shoulders, and the well was deep and the water was cold. So there was this little girl, being drenched with bucket after bucket of icy cold water. Momma was trying to unmat her hair, and get all the hay, new and used, out of her thick hair. Then Momma bathed her in that same cold water, and Nola Ruth never walked on that side of the barn again.

## Cow Chips

"Hey Mickey, let's go across the road to the west pasture and throw cow chips," called Ross.

"What are cow chips?" I asked.

"Well they're just cow chips. Come on, I'll show you; it's a lot of fun," said Ross.

Now farm kids like to play tricks on city kids. Not mean tricks, just the kind of things to let the city kids know that they don't know everything. And the Randall kids had a bag full of tricks to pull on their city cousins.

This is about a particularly unique farm activity that's known as flipping cow chips. City kids and cow chips are strangers to each other. Until they've spent some time on a farm, city kids have never even heard of cow chips. Nola Ruth and I, therefore, were easy targets for our country cousins, who were more than willing to teach us all about cow chips.

Just to set the record straight: cow chips are cow droppings that when hitting the ground just flatten out into disks. When the disks dry out, they become hardened little frisbees. Our country cousins played games of throwing them at each other.

At the start of the game, Ross, Delores and Lester would give Nola Ruth and I the cow chips. But it didn't take long, as a game went on, before Ross said, "hand me that chip over there."

And guess what? Those chips, although they all looked dry, some are not completely dry. As I turned and picked up the chip, it squished in my hands. I looked at Ross. He, Delores and Lester were laughing their heads-off; and I had all this cow chip, oozing between my fingers.

I did not find it funny at the time. I vowed to get even. They would be in the city one day, and they would get theirs. We ran over to a little creek that flowed through the field and washed off our hands.

Ross really was not very nice. He couldn't stop laughing. He was that kind of a guy, who loved to see somebody get in trouble or to play jokes on them. Fifty years later he is still the same way.

After the cow chips, we walked through the cornfields and bean fields. We saw rabbits and squirrels. We flushed up pheasants and quails. Lester showed us where there were some fox traps. We found crab apple trees and ate crab apples. We told Ross we had them in the city also. They showed us where they picked wild grapes and raspberries and blackberries. And we just walked around the fields and woods. Lester had a pocket watch. He looked at it and said it was getting on to supper time. So we better be getting back to the house.

I don't remember what we had for supper except biscuits that melted in your mouth and homemade butter. I mean farm-made butter. The Randall family love to drink buttermilk. Nola Ruth and I were not accustomed to drinking buttermilk.

After supper, there were even more farm chores. The city kids discovered that on a farm there was always work to do and that Ross and Delores also had chores.

They had to make certain the chickens were all in the coop. They helped slop the hogs. That's feeding the hogs for city folks. They helped clean up the barn, sweeping and moving around things. We were not aware of what they were doing most of the time. But they were busy and still playing.

After the barn, we went to the water pump and drank from the big dipper hanging by the pump. For city kids to do that, we thought it was cool, real neat, a pleasure. As for the water, it was cold.

Darkness is beginning to creep upon us, and we had to get sleeping areas and arrangements together. Also the children had to have their bedtime snack. That bedtime snack was a bowl of buttermilk with bread, biscuits or cornbread, whichever was available.

The buttermilk had flecks of real butter floating around. It was a lot differently than the gooey stuff you see in stores nowadays. I did not like buttermilk then. But I do like real farm fresh buttermilk today. When you get older, you appreciate those things, that as a child you didn't like.

Aunt Lillian and Uncle Coy were coming to the county that weekend, so the kids were to sleep in the loft, on pallets on the floor. We thought that was cool. We really enjoyed that. So we made pallets of blankets and sheets, pillows and straw pillows, and drowned and covered ourselves in the blankets; and proceeded to talk most of the night till we fell asleep. And as soon as we were asleep, it was time to wake up.

We repeated this day exactly the same way, but different, for six days. As you can tell, the city kids really liked that trip very much. Very, very much.

In that summer of '49.

I still remember.

# GIRLS

*Girls and more*

You may have noted, by now, not too much mention has been made of girls. That's because an 11 year old boy doesn't really have too much to do with girls. At least, this 11 year old boy didn't know too much about girls. I found out later that I was a little slower than most of the boys around. Some say I'm still slow.

There was my first sweetheart, when I was in kindergarten, and she was in nursery school. When you talk about puppy love, that was real puppy love. Many years later (I won't say how many years), I was surprised, and pleasantly so, to find that she still remembered that I was her first boy friend. But outside of that I was clean until the fifth grade.

How can I ever forget that fling? It was just at the beginning of the summer of '49, when school was letting out. I had fallen hard for her. There were those brown eyes that held me transfixed, when she looked at me. She had a whisper in her voice that fascinated me. She was the one for me; I just knew it.

We pretended that there was nothing between us. We thought we had it covered, but everyday at recess, the class would have big fun, by letting us know that they knew.

How could they know? We were trying so hard to be secretive. Like, when I would leave to go to my safety patrol post, I would secretly put a note on her desk as I passed by. We thought that no one saw it. Of course, everybody in the classroom saw it, but we were being cool. We were sweethearts for almost two weeks, maybe three.

Now let me go on record, with one indisputable fact! Girls at this age are tom boys, and they can hold their own with any boy their age. In fact, they attack most boys their age, and dare the boys to do anything about it.

My sweetheart was from a large family of nine or eleven, or something like that, and was very much accustomed to getting or fighting to get her way. She was always determined to win one way or the other. In other words, she was a tough little momma. But I didn't know that at the time.

I don't know what happened. But something happened that made her mad at me; but for no reason she attacked me. She beat the devil out of me. That was on Monday. On Tuesday she beat the devil back into me.

I was the laughing stock of the class. A girl was beating me, and I couldn't do anything about it. I could do nothing except take the lumps.

She skipped Wednesday. But Thursday, I apparently made some smart remark, and I got beat again. I lost the fight, but I was getting better.

Then came Friday. I was walking along minding my own business, and I was attacked from the rear. She jumped on my back, and we rolled over into the little ditch, next-to the dirt road. With snow suits (well so it wasn't near summer; it was late spring and still cold in Michigan. I just forgot about the time. But since we've gone this far, I'll finish this snap shot) and mitts, tangled and dirty, we tumbled and fought.

But this time I won the fight. I could now hold my head high and proudly look my buddies in the eye. I had conquered that girl. I continued walking home feeling good about myself. I got home and cleaned and washed up. I helped Momma set the table, and sat down with the family to enjoy a very good dinner or supper as we called it in those days.

Then the doorbell rang. If I had known what awaited me on the other side of that door, I would've immediately left home and joined the circus. To become a roustabout for the rest of my life, and giving up all hope of ever seeing friends or family and loved ones again. It would've been a great sacrifice, but it would've been worth it rather than opening that door.

Now understand that all week long, I went home hiding busted lips and bloody noses from Momma and Grandma. I even told them I didn't remember how my jacket pocket got torn. But back to the doorbell.

There stood Rev. Sam. He stood very, very tall. Here was a man with fire in his eyes. Now understand, Rev. Sam and my Grandma, didn't sit on the same pew in regards to lifestyles. Rev. Sam was on one side of the moral fence of life, and Grandma was on the fence. So the fact that the reverend had come to our house underscored the seriousness of his complaint and the tenuous hold on life that I had.

Rev. Sam's frame filled the doorway. He was menacing. Sunday school visions and pictures of avenging angels best described his appearance and my fear.

Beside him, almost lost in his coat that engulfed him was a shaking bundle with legs. It was a little crying, whimpering girl. She looked pitiful. She appeared dazed and lost. Her snowsuit was dirty, her hair was straggly, and tears were falling from her eyes like buckets of rainwater.

No, don't tell me. This could not be the tom boy. This could not be the same little girl that had been beating me up all week. But it was. My mouth and eyes were wide open in disbelief. There she was with her father, putting on that big crying act for my mother and grandmother.

Years later I learned the act was necessary in order to save her own little behind. It came down to either her behind or my life. I lost.

Why is it that, it is always "years later," when the truth comes out; or some girl tells you that if you had done, "such and such," you could have gotten "such and such."

Rev. Sam glared and said, "see what your son did to my daughter."

My mother turned and looked at me with a look that I will never forget.

She asked, "Were you fighting a girl?"

I said, "No mother, she was fighting me. She's been beating me up all week long. Today was the first day she lost."

Again, mother asked, "Were you fighting a girl?"

At this point. I knew it was best for me not to say anything else.

There was no Miranda Rule in those days, but I was smart enough to know, that if I didn't say anything else, they couldn't hang me with my own words. Oh there was going to be a hanging, but not with my words helping.

"Go to your room," mother said.

She turned and made the correct apologies to Rev. Sam and said that she would see to it that this would never happen again. About that she was right!

You have already discovered by reading this book so far that corporal punishment was considered an acceptable form of discipline for children, when I was a child. Spare the rod and spoil the child, just didn't happen then.

I don't remember what the family had to eat for dinner that night. I think the dinner was pretty glum after our visitors left. Everyone ate though, but of course, I didn't eat anything. I was in my room, trying to find enough sheets to tie together to escape out the window. But it was dark by now, and I was afraid of dark. Besides, I knew I had to be home when the street lights came on; and they were already on.

Sometime later, mother came to my room. She was shaking her head in disbelief and saying over and over to herself, "You were fighting a girl."

I tried explaining that she had been jumping on me and beating me up all week long. I was just defending myself. She'd given me a bloody nose and busted lips. She had torn my jacket pocket the other day when I told you, I didn't know how it happened. That was a wrong thing to say.

Mother, she was just shaking her head and saying over and over, "You were fighting a girl."

She was not listening to me anymore because I was not a part of her world anymore.

"You were fighting a girl."

I wished she would stop saying that. She was not really a girl. She was a tom boy's tom boy. She was always beating up everybody.

Mother, just shook her head, and said, "You were fighting a girl."

She then proceeded to give me the worse whipping I had had before or since in my life.

And even to this day, when I see this old fifth grade sweetheart, I still remind her on that day, and the pain she caused me to suffer.

So as you can see, my experience with girls was not that good. I discovered, many years later, that other guys were having fun with girls. I never got to that point. I guess I really was slow.

## The Sisters for Life

### *They All Became Sisters*

These are the girls that you grew up with from grade school on into adulthood. They became and will always be your best buddies. These are your sister, sisters for life.

They started out being just little girls with skinny legs, plats, braids and pigtails. You played with them at recess in games called, "Red Rover Red Rover," let Charlie come over. But whenever they called, it was always Duff or Clyde or Roosevelt. They never called Mickey. That was OK. When we got down to the end of bodies, they'd call me.

These are the sisters that get away with more things, on or to you than anybody else. You will do things for them because you have a special kind of love for them.

Many times it's because you don't want to hear their mouth or complaints. You don't want them to talk about you, but they will. And when they decide to get on your case, there's nothing you can do about it.

They have no problem telling you, "I don't care who you are now Mr. Big Shot. I knew you when you were nothin' but a runny nose cry baby. So don't get so high and mighty with me."

Even our wives, unless they grew up in Saginaw, don't understand this strange "Saginaw thing" we people have. They tell us nobody else acts like you Saginaw fools.

And the wives are right. I have not noticed this kind of

entanglement in other groups of people to the extent that the "Sagnasty" folks display their strange kinship. I have noticed a similar bond between the, "Saginaw Valley" folks of Pontiac, Flint, and Bay City and the people from Lansing. We all were caught in that time frame, where we were a very small minority and had to learn how to fit into a so-called open society.

Those of us who grew up in that small-town in the forties, fifties and sixties,—Black, White, or Mexican—all acknowledge that there is a special kind of bond that unites us. I don't mean to get serious right now, so I'll move on.

Other people, may challenge the manner in which I try to exalt the bonds of Saginaw's togetherness, and uniqueness, above all others. And it's fair for those folks to take issue with me. I not going to fight them.

But lets get back to what sisters can make you do. It is because of one of those sisters that I went to a reunion that I did not want to go. However; I did not want to hear sister, Sister's mouth even more. So I went, and I met my present wife. We had known each other since the third grade but had walked to the beat of different drummers. But we met again at the reunion and had it not been for the fear of listening to Sister's mouth, I would have missed a very wonderful and beautiful, life experience.

### It happened this way

Girls would chase their favorite little boys (nobody ever chased me). One particular girl ran after my best buddy; and when she got to him, naturally, I had to help my buddy. That little girl turned and looked at me and gave me a mean look. She was a little skinny girl, and that mean look made her eyes become little slits. Her lips clenched and became invisible. But one look at her and I said to myself, she was a mean little girl. I am not going to have anything to do with her.

Now understand, all through grade school, junior high school and high school, I never said more than a dozen words to this girl. I did not dislike her, and she didn't dislike me. She was just some person I knew. She never did anything to me, and I never did anything to her. We just did not hang out with the same group of people.

She and I were in the same grade. And when you got pass grade school, girls did not like boys their age or in the same grade. Therefore, in her mind, I did not exist.

We went our separate ways in life after school and never saw each other again, until that high school reunion some thirty-five years later. She was a widow, and I for the first time was without a date. Therefore, I also needed some one to pick on. Oh well, she was fresh meat and got stuck. She tried to tell me that I didn't want to mess with her and that I couldn't handle her. The nerve of that woman by this time in life I was no longer slow. It was only because I was taking a break that she even got a chance to say hello. Well I showed her, and at the next reunion when we said we were getting married, it surprised most everyone.

Grace spent the next years saying, "Iola and Charlie? Charlie and Iola?" Even now, she still can't believe it.

There I hope that's a good cleanup, Sister. OK?

So today, now older, all of us who grew up together in the same neighborhood, in the same classes, are sisters and brothers. We cherish each other. We love each other. There is this sticky, clinging string that forever ties us together

And about that whipping—you know, the worst whipping of my life because of my fifth grade sweetheart— this was still a good time.

It was still a great summer, that summer of '49.

I still remember.

# A DAY IN THE LIFE

A day in the life of an 11-year-old boy does not start that morning he wakes up. Naw it starts way back when he was a kid. Like somewhere between crawling and talking, he discovers that there is a difference between boys and girls, and it is more than just on the physical plane.

He finds it is no longer cute for him to spray somebody when they change his diaper. It becomes very uncomfortable and downright bothersome to have his hair combed each day. And what is it with this ritual about the first haircut? Mother and father proudly take the little lamb for his first shearing.

To fathers, it is the passage from infancy to boyhood, so now he can really start teaching him about becoming a man.

To mothers, it is one less wailing, thankless, fight in the morning. She was tired of fighting that boy about combing or fixing his hair.

To the boy it was just somebody else messing with his head, and he don't like it.

Then gradually bit by bit, all the soft cuddly toys are taken away. Oh, he may be allowed to keep an old towel or blanket, and maybe, even an old teddy bear. But that will be about it.

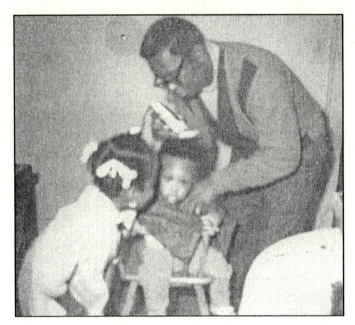

*The first hair cut of my son. As you can see, he did not like it. It has been the same for all boys at any time. Tatie, Charlie IV's 7 year old sister; Charlie IV at 1 year old; me struggling with the clippers.*

Slowly he learns that he is different from girls. By the time he can run fast enough to fall and scrape his knees, he is aware of the fact that those other little people are things called girls. And he doesn't know why, but he's not one and does not want to be one of them.

By the time he can talk in sentences, he really doesn't like playing with girls, well some girls, because they are too soft and cry too easily; and they're just like his sisters and brothers always, tellin' Momma that he did it.

He is different—that must be good because Daddy and Mommy smile so broadly and proudly, when they tell him that he is different than girls.

This growing up to be a boy thing is scatter gun crazy. You just learn to do things. There are no real rules, guidelines or classes. You just learn that men do certain things, and women do other things; and since you're going to be a man, you do a lot of doing man-type things, whatever that means.

You start developing habits and doing things differently. Take bedrooms, for example; normally you're not too worried about how the room looks. Why make up your bed every morning? It'll only get messed up again that night. Why not sleep on top of the bed and the next morning it's all made up? Mothers and girls don't seem to understand this kind of logic.

And boys are naturally more curious about garter snakes and toads, pulling the legs off spiders, and catching grasshoppers And boy, do you feel good when your right jab's fast enough to catch flies in midair. These are things a man really has to know.

Mothers may insist that you learn things like how to wash dishes. Mother will make you set the table and put the knives and forks on the correct side of the plate. Some will make you learn how to clean house and cook and wash dishes. It seemed like I was always washing dishes. I hated washing dishes, and it seemed like Nola Ruth never washed dishes.

Somewhere along the way of growing up, girls changed again. Maybe it's a instinctive thing. Girls became neat and clean freaks. Face, hair, clothes, shoes, even skinny legs, have to be neat and clean.

But it's really about clothes. Clothes are all that girls think about (I didn't learn until I was way past grown, that those little girls were also thinking about boys. Like I said, I was slow.). Their little dresses always had to be neat and clean. Their little pants, I mean, slacks were pressed neatly. They couldn't be dirty or have holes in them. And they had cute little hankies for runny noses, or else they carried tissues.

A girl had to have her hair combed out or braided, tied up in ribbons or rubber bands, and it took them forever.

She had to put lotion on her face and put hand lotion on her hands; and she put lotion or Vaseline on her little skinny legs so they wouldn't look so white and ashy.

Now it was easy for a boy to comb his hair because our hair was normally cut very short. And we made certain that we found the biggest comb in the house, with the biggest teeth, and with two passes, we were done.

But with boys that clothes stuff didn't matter that much. I didn't like having holes in the knees of my bib overalls, because I was on my knees a lot: shooting marbles, playing ball, or getting snagged climbing a fence that I should not have been climbing anyway. So therefore, I had holes in the knees of my pants. Knee holes didn't bother me too much, although sometimes I used safety pins to close them up a little. I just didn't want holes in the front and center, or splits on the back side of my pants, for sure.

And shirts, well, there was an undershirt and something on top of that most times. If we wore another shirt, it might be buttoned all the way except for the cuff buttons.

Shirt sleeve cuffs were always good to have, especially for wiping your nose. And they were also good for trying to do magic tricks, like flipping quarters up your sleeve or hiding cards. These tricks didn't fool anyone; everybody tried to do them, even the girls.

Socks and shoes were also a loose requirement. The socks were clean enough, as long as they weren't too stiff. I had only one pair of weekday shoes to worry about; but even then, I kept losing one of them.

As you get a little older, you become more defensive about playing with girls. At least that's how I felt back then, but I was slow. You don't play pick up sticks or ball and jacks with girls, unless there are no fellows around and even then you appear to be bored and uninterested.

You didn't play hopscotch with girls when there were fellows around unless you wanted to make points with the new girl. I never played hopscotch. I was even slow in getting to the new girls.

As you can see, this was and is not a science...growing up and learning how to be a boy. There are as many rules about the process, as there are mothers and fathers.

Some of my ideas about being a man got stuck in my head when I was in the first and second grade. We were living on the south side of town then. Our next-door neighbor, Mr. Buddy, was a boxer and had been a number one middleweight contender once. He had also worked in the circus and knew some trapeze tricks. So naturally, Mr. Buddy taught me trapeze tricks and how to box. Along the way he also taught me what his idea of a man was. At that age I was like a sponge; I soaked up everything. It was fun listening to him talk about things that he used to do.

But the main things that Mr. Buddy taught me about being a man was you have to take care of your home. You had go out and to get what you wanted, you had to hustle.

He would say, "Mickey, don't sleep all day like a woman. Get up and do something even if it's to get dressed and walk around the block. A man's got to find something to do with himself. Get out of the house and hustle."

Ladies and girls, before you take my head off, understand I did not say you slept all day. This is what I was told as a young boy, many years ago as a prod to make me do something. That's what Mr. Buddy said, and he didn't mean it literally, or word for word; it was just an expression. We all know how good women make great contributions to the family. And they do not sleep all day or even half a day, I don't think.

Anyway, moving on, in my case, that all boiled down to one thing. I had to stop sleeping so much and get out of bed in the morning. For me, that was the real hard task. But that was the requirement. I didn't know if I'd ever be that kind of a man, but because Mr. Buddy said so, I tried

So we have the background to understand, a day in the life of this 11-year-old boy.

### The Day Begins

Geez oh man, the sun's up already. I guess I'd better get up and out. Like the cowboys say, we're burning daylight.

I'd better get up and get dressed before everybody else does. I hope I don't wake grandma; she'll find a million things for me to do. Nothing will wake up Nola Ruth.

I think I'll sneak over to Miss Polly's house to steal some Jitterbug's plums. I don't know what else I'll do right after that.

Boy, are these plums good. They're still cool from the morning dew, and they're juicy and sweet. Oops, I'm getting juice all over my shirt. Just biting these things makes the juice run all down my chin and drips all over the front of my shirt.

Ah shucks, Momma's gonna get me for wiping my chin off on my shirt sleeve. Oh well, the shirt had stains on it anyway.

Very early in the morning, I'd get up, get dressed, and go sit on the porch or walk up to the corner. Sometimes I'd go across the street to Miss Polly's backyard and steal plums from her tree. Of course it was not a real theft, because she knew I was there and her son knew I was there; the whole neighborhood knew I was there. But anyway, it was fun pretending I was getting away with something.

Oh boy, today is Thursday and tomorrow is Friday; RB and I would have to go over to Miss Queen's house and a few other places to cut the grass. We'll probably make two dollars, each of us.

We had a grass cutting business. A few people took pity on us and let us cut their grass on the weekends

During the winter months, we emptied ashes from people's stoves and furnaces and spread it over the ice and snow on steps and sidewalks. Why buy a whole lot of salt when ashes are almost free? Besides it was mostly too cold for the salt to melt the ice anyway.

RB is a lifelong buddy from the third grade. His Grandmother and my mother would tell our teachers at the beginning of each school year—despite both our last names starting with a "B"—do not sit us together or close by each other.

And each year the dumb teachers would say that they could handle it. And each year after the second week, I was sitting in one corner on the front row and RB was sitting in the opposite corner in the back row. He got the back row because he was and is sneakier than I was; and he had this fake good boy image going on.

He was raised by his grandfather, the pastor, of that big church on Sixth Street. However, his Grandmother and my mother developed a warm and understanding friendship. Momma was very active in the church and was known not to be a part of the family business like Grandma. She was proud that she shielded her children from being involved in worldly activities of the neighborhood.

But anyway, R.B. could come to my house just about any time. There he learned of fine art of playing old maid, pitty-pat and tonk. Our favorite game was a Parker Brother's game that I can't find, called "Worldwide Treasure Hunt." A game that taught us all about geography and treasures around the world.

As I said in the beginning, we still wonder, like how we went from taking out ashes to being engineers and pharmacists. We just did somethin' and hustled.

After raiding Jitterbug's yard, I'd walk back to my house and walk around the yard, looking at the freshness of the morning glories and the pansies. Snipping the blossoms of the orange flags, intermingled with the multi-colored irises, I'd go along sucking out the sweet nectar of the flower, while always being careful not to snip too many as to cause Momma to complain.

At times I'd find myself smelling the roses and chasing away the bees. Then turn running and being chased away by the bees. I liked the roses. The pink, white, and the little yellow ones were OK, but I most loved the blood red American Beauties roses.

Then the tulips of late spring or early summer always caught my attention. There were the tulips: red and small and big. Some were purple or white or primary yellow or "Cadillac pink" tulips.

On other days getting up the morning meant walking around the neighborhood or taking long walks. On some ambitious Saturdays, I'd ask Momma if I could go (to go meant to walk) to the south side to see Willie Jeff. It was quite a walk of several miles. I don't know how many, but it was a long way.

I'd walk by the duplex house on Gilmore street where we used to live and where I used to hang by my knees on the trapeze. One day, at lunch time, I decided to do some quick swings and flips. I don't know what happened. I only remember being carried into the house. I didn't go back to school that afternoon.

There was the house of a girl called Mary. Her dad was a cowboy, and she often acted so superior to us, just because her dad was once a cowboy; our dads were just plain old factory workers.

While walking to Willie Jeff's street, I remembered a lot of things. I liked living on the South Side. By the time I got to my buddy's house, he was out, sitting on the porch.

We'd go walking, or we'd play catch in the field or at the Naval Reserve Armory. Most of the time we made something out of doing nothing at all. It was fun being together and is still fun to see each other nowadays

Another fun thing to do early in the morning in late spring was to walk the little ditches by Potter School. The ditches were still filled with icy cold water, and we'd be wading. Of course we're not supposed to get in the water; but what did that have to do with anything. We were busy about the business of catching crawfish or crayfish. We'd get the little things and wonder how people could eat them. They were too small. We said it must be some other kind of crawfish, because these did not look very appetizing, you know, or good to eat.

Just "wondering" took up most of the morning. And around lunch time, you'd be hungry. So I'd find a way back home, unless I had enough pennies and a couple of nickels. Then I'd get a candy bar and maybe a bag of potato chips. And you always knew of a few backyards that still had a water pump, if you got thirsty.

But if you were broke, bologna sandwiches and hot dogs, or peanut butter sandwiches, awaited you at home; that is if you fixed them yourself. We normally had an ample supply of salami, the kind with the big peppercorns and a heavy garlic flavor. I became tired of salami. But I like it now.

So with a sandwich or two in one hand and a glass of milk in the other hand, I'd find my favorite tree stump in the backyard and start eating and day dreaming. Of course, those were short dreams, because the sandwiches were gone rather quickly.

It was by design that I went to the backyard, because staying in the kitchen or going to the front porch, meant that I was in the line of sight of Grandma or Momma...and that could mean work. You know Manual Labor my closest friend. I had learned years ago, that if I kept a low profile, Grandma would overlook me or forget that she wanted me most of the time. However, that did not work with Momma. She may over look you, but she would never forget that she wanted you.

After finishing the sandwiches and milk, I'd knock down some of the ripest green apples on the tree in the backyard. They were so sour, they would lock up your jaws. Then I'd try to slip away on the far side of the yard along the mulberry trees. If I was sneaky enough, I'd run up to the corner of Fourth Street and see if Donald was free to play. Or I'd run into one of the Scotts or some other guys, and we'd cross Washington Street to go over behind the Leather Tannery Plant, where a lot of the kids used to swim. I never did swim there because the water didn't look right.

Once on the other side of Washington, we'd walk up and down the old abandoned railroad tracks: talking, throwing rocks, trying to hit rabbits, or squirrels in trees or on telephone poles. And of course, we were always looking for snakes.

Every now and then, we'd find empty pop and beer bottles and would fight over who saw it first. We'd cross Washington again at

Fifth, and go see if Poochie was home.

Sometimes across the street on the corner of Farwell and Fifth at the vacant lot next to Kenneth Holmes Barber Shop and next to the hole in the ground Church or blind pig (I can't agree with my historical resource, my wife, so we'll leave it this way), a local welterweight pro boxer named Billy would have a boxing ring set up and be training. That always attracted a good-size crowd, and he got to show off and demonstrate what a real flashy fighter he was. I never did know how good his record was.

Between rounds while he was jumping rope or doing something else, little kids, like myself and others, would jump in the ring and pretend we were boxing each other. The crowd used to laugh their heads off at us. It was great fun. A few years later, when I thought I was very good, I got into the ring with Billy. I landed a clean good body blow, and he chased me around the ring flashing a left jab inches from my face for about 5 seconds. It was a good thing I knew how to back pedal and duck and weave.

He said it was all right, he wasn't going to hurt me. I'm glad he knew that because I didn't

It's funny how young kids stay hungry. Since I was just across the street from the house, I felt it was safe enough to slip in a get another sandwich. But Momma saw me this time.

"I've been looking for you," she said. "Run down to Jerry's and get a loaf of bread and a package he's holding for me."

The package happened to be Philip Morris cigarettes. That was her brand in those days. Shucks, that was easy. I thought I had to do some real work. So I ran to Jerry's food market, picked up the bread and package, and ran back home. I dropped off the things on the dining room table and ran out before she could think of something else

The rest of the afternoon was spent walking around, playing catch, stick ball, shooting marbles, and a whole lot of other stuff.

And before you knew it, it was supper time. I had to come in, wash up, and most of the time, I had to put on a clean shirt because my other shirt was too dirty for me to sit at the table and eat.

After supper, I'd go down to Norman Street and watch the ladies softball team practice. Mr. Eight Ball was always there coaching the women. He along with some other members of the Saginaw Eagles were always on hand.  They were good coaches, and the team was a good team.

But before long, it was getting dark, and the street lights were about to come on.  That meant we had to get home, and that one of our favorite radio programs was about to come on.

By this time it was normally eight o'clock or 8:30 in the evening and that meant that soon I would be sound asleep.

There you have it.  A very exciting, thrilling, and most of all, fun-filled, typical day in the life of 11-year-old boy in the summer of '49.

I still remember.

# TROOP 15 THE BOY SCOUTS

Boom Boom  you play too much man.
Look ouuu.........ttt!!!!!!!!

The next thing I remember is sliding down the stairs, head first, on my stomach.  Unlike today, I did not have so much stomach; so catching the top of those steps were my little hip bones, the only things big enough on me to stick out.

I reached the bottom of the stairs in pain, with tears running down my face, and of course, nobody knew what or how it happened.  I was just the victim of an unfortunate accident.  Nobody caused it.  I was just an unlucky kid.  Nobody was around me.  I was all by myself.  Although there were 15 guys, pushing and shoving at the top of the stairs, I was alone, as usual, in those days.  So lets you and I start at the beginning of what it was like to be in Boy Scout Troop 15.  It really was a lot of fun.

Had it not been for Donny, I would've missed telling you about the adventures of Troop 15.  Troop 15 was the last Boy Scout troop to be formed in our part of town.  When troops 16 and 17 (I think it was 17) organized, there were still some boys left over.  So the Elks Club decided to sponsor the new troop, and it was called Troop 15.

We used to meet on the second-floor of the Elks Club on Potter Street.

So since we were the newest troop in scouting, the boys in the other troops, attempted to make us the brunt of many jokes and pranks. But we were not about to have any of that. We fought back and gave better than we got. Troop 16 was our biggest or most intense rival.

Yep, the other troops thought they were better than we were. But our troop leader and scout master, TJ, was determined to make us as good as the other two Boy Scout Troops. So at each meeting we'd work on things to earn our merit badges and all the other Boy Scout stuff. Afterwards, we'd work on marching and fancy drilling and got to be as good as troops 16 or 17.

We never did catch up with them in Explorer and Eagle Scouts, because by that age our guys were no longer just interested in Explorer or Eagle scouting. Most of our older scouts were earning merit badges in scouting girls and capture (years later we learned that the girls did the capturing). How little I knew. I was still trying to earn real merit badges. I was slow.

It was a special treat for our troop to spend a weekend at the Kiwanis Club Boy Scout camp. For scouts it was one of our "mostest" fun things to do. The troop would be put up in a cabin that was big enough to hold about 10 or 15 fellows. There was a fireplace, a kitchen area and a bedroom for the scout master and staff. The rest of the rooms were the latest up-to-date facilities and were provided with two holes. Paper was always a precious commodity, so each individual tried to remember to bring his own.

One June weekend when we went to the camp, it turned out to be cold, cold and then cold. The weekend did not start out that way, but that's Michigan for you. We had not expected a cold weekend so we brought only light spring clothing and Boy Scout shirts. We each had a blanket and a couple pair of socks and that was about it.

The weekend started out being warm and sunny. That Friday afternoon when we arrived was perfect. But as the sun went down, it got damp, cool, uncomfortable and cold. The weather changed but that's Michigan for you.

Around nine o'clock Friday night, after the sun had been down for a while and we were tired of our games of throwing spit balls, socks and other things, we started feeling uncomfortable.

Then we gradually noticed it was getting cold. Some guys were putting their pants on over their pajama bottoms. Others put shirts on top of their pajama tops, or whatever we had that we were sleeping in. Next came the putting on of two pair of socks and doubling up our blankets. Some guys were doubling up and using both the blankets together. This was getting serious.

Our scoutmaster TJ looked around outside and found the cabin's fireplace log stash. He started to try and build a fire in the fireplace, but it was plugged. So he started a fire in our potbelly stove. He got that stove cherry red hot.

After TJ got that little potbelly stove going, we sat around the stove and started telling ghost stories. TJ, his assistant, and the senior scouts did the story telling. They tricked us into listening to all those tall tale ghost stories.

The stories started as safety lessons on being careful in the woods and how you can get lost, never to be found again. Be careful they'd say. Don't go to the outhouse by yourself. That was the second most dangerous place at night. Be careful on how you mark your trail, because sometimes markers and signs got lost or turned around.

"T J, do you remember that little Joswenson boy? You know that German and Swedish kid who had that real white, white, sickly lookin' skin?" asked Boom Boom.

"Yeah I remember. He was so ashamed of being so white that he always went to the john by himself. Now what happened to him?" asked T J.

"You know what happened. He went to the outhouse one night. In fact he sneaked out of the cabin. He went by himself, and he didn't tell anybody he was gone. You know what happened to him all right," said Mr. Charles Couch, another scout master (he and his wife Miss Sabra were life long close friends to all the family).

With that the instigators, the scout leaders, turned away and pretended to look for pork and beans and marshmallows and just left 15 boys with wide-open eyes and mouths wondering about what happened?

"What happened?" we all yelled.

"I don't want to talk about it," said Boom Boom.

"What happened? As we all jumped Boom Boom and pinned him to the cold damp floor. We were enjoying this part."

"T J, tell them," gurgled our captive. Some body had him in a choke hold. We were enjoying this part.

"You tell them. I wasn't goin' bring up that boy, but you and your big mouth got you in another mess," said T J.

At that moment Boom-Boom made a big lurch to get free. A few of us went flying, and he almost got to his knees. But we were right back on him.

"Are you gonna' talk?" We sneared through clenched teeth. We were enjoying this part.

"Come on guys, enough is enough," screamed the fallen big Eagle scout.

"Give him a break fellas," said Mr. Couch.

"There is really not much to tell. The boy wasn't missed until the next morning. We searched for days, but we never found him. We didn't find his clothes, his knapsack, his body, not even his toilet paper. It sure was strange, nothing," said Mr. Couch.

"But sometimes at night, it seems to be as though he's heard crying out, and people would go looking for him...and they would get lost. At other times they were found and they'd have a blank look on their faces," continued Mr. Couch.

And before you know it, we were into telling real live ghost stories. We were eating it up. Knowing all about how the stories could not be real and how we could not be scared by the stories; yet at the same time, wondering whether or not they were true.

So there we were, huddling around that potbelly stove, burning up on the frontside and freezing off our backside. We spent most of the night around that potbelly stove looking at each other and at TJ, Mr. Couch and Boom Boom. The three of them captivating each of our little and wild imaginations.

After a while the stove changed color from being a cherry red to dark dusty faded rose. We retreated to our bunks and to sleeping till morning.

Boom-Boom deserved his name. He shattered the morning by yelling at the top and bottom of his voice, and waking up everybody. We had to wash up and skip taking a shower, because there was no hot water in the camp. The water was ice cold.

The guys in the line up at the outhouse were freezing. Some of the guys inside were really rushing their business. Then there were others who were too slow. They were inside shivering and freezing, while trying not to get stuck in the holes.

Since there were no indoor toilet seats, you always brought plenty of toilet paper to spread around. The paper served many functions. When you ran out of your private stash of paper, you would be surprised at what leaves and newspapers can do. This particular morning we were all OK for toilet paper.

Meanwhile the Scout leaders and the Eagle and Explorer scouts were fixing breakfast. They had prepared mounds of hash brown American fried potatoes and onions, and that was a lot of frying. There were lots of scrambled eggs with stove top and skillet toast. We had bacon and bacon and I don't want to forget we had bacon. And naturally for growing, clean, loyal, brave (and the rest of that motto) boys, there was plenty of milk.

After fussin', scheming and trying avoid it, we got the breakfast mess and the cabin cleaned up. Then the rest of the day was ours. We ran through the woods, and identified trees, bushes and birds. We imitated bird calls, pretended we were Indians, and tracked our Scout leaders as they made trails, that even Stevie Wonder could see (he's the Hall of Fame singer, whose grandmother lived next door to our family).

Every now and then we'd see a Boy Scout Troop from the other side of town. We'd play with them or say hello for a little while, and then we'd all go our separate ways. Most of those troops had been scouting for years and were better equipped or organized than we were, but we were having just as much fun as those kids were.

By lunch time, we'd find our way back to our cabin. For lunch I really don't remember what we had, except I know it had to be hot dogs and pork and beans. Sometimes for a change up, we'd have pork and beans and cut-up hot dogs along with light bread. Notice it was light bread and not white bread. But we consumed cans and cans of pork and beans. More importantly sooner or later, your nose would know. After lunch we went home. We were not about to freeze another night.

During the course of the summer there were Saginaw Valley Boy Scout parades and neighborhood parades in which we would march and display our skills. We would go on paper drives to collect newspapers for whatever reason they were used. From time to time we would be at various churches as an example to other young boys and girls of the good work that the Boy Scouts did in making us better citizens and in keeping us out of trouble. Well they were mostly right; few of us ever got caught at anything and most became fairly good citizens.

We had as much fun going home from scout meetings, as we did at the meeting. Most of the guys lived on the other side of the tracks but several others, like myself, lived on the good side of the tracks. Going home after a meeting we played a game called Green Leaves. You had to always have a "green tree leave" with you—or be the victim of a hard punch to the upper arm. The leaf had to be in recognizable condition. No pieces or fragments could save you. Later it became fresh green leaf; thus dried leaves in your wallet were no good. Now if someone guessed wrong and hit you and you had a green leaf, you could give10 free punches to his shoulder. I think it was 10 punches. I forget how many. You'll have to ask RB or Donny about the rules of retaliation.

Another thing on the way home from Boy Scout meetings, we could raid various backyards for plum, cherry, peach, mulberry, apple, pear or crabapple trees all over town. Everybody seemed to be growing something or have a fruit tree in their backyard. Some owners approved, and we knew just about where everyone of them was. We knew how to get in and out again, with the least amount of inconvenience to ourselves or to the householder. After all, we did not want them to become upset or too anxious to catch us stealing their fruit. It's one thing to have one boy taking an apple or two, but when you've got about 10 boys stealing apples, you don't have any apples left

Guys on my side of town lived farthest from the Elks Club, so therefore, we had more opportunities to enjoy the fruits of our neighbors or put another way, we had more chances to get caught.

If it wasn't too dark after scout meeting, we'd stop at the playground on Third and Norman. We'd play basketball or baseball with the kids there and then hurry home.

Next time I'll get Donny or Lunk to tell you more about what we got into as members of Boy Scout Troop 15.

I don't recall anything else special that we did that summer.

It was just another fun part of the summer of '49.

I still remember.

# GOOD BYE OLD PAINT

"Good bye Old Paint"—that's cowboy talk for when their horse dies. So I said the same to the family's old steed, "Good bye Old Paint," our now lonesome and blue '36 Dodge.

In the spring of 1949, it was with mixed feelings that we finally laid to rest the old '36 Dodge. It departed from us with dignity and with its head held high, as it was towed around the corner to Mr. Honey Dripper's garage. We watched it go, with tears forming in the corner of our eyes. It had been so much fun, looking at the road through the holes in the floor, or looking at the night sky through the roof holes. There would be no more shaking to the flapping of the fenders, and that special rattle of the bolted on bumpers as we crossed the rail road tracks. Nola Ruth and I had become quite attached to that car.

But I really must be honest, we were happy to get a new car. Grandma and Momma had bought a new Nash Ambassador. (Nash Car Company, bought the Jeep Co. and became American Motors, which was bought by Chrysler Co. which was bought by Mercedes Benz). The car was kind of a lime type, yellow, with a dark brown top. The '49 Nash Ambassador looked like a duck's back and tail end. But it was a brand new car, and had four doors with no holes in the floor or roof. And a wonderful feature was that the front seats could fold backwards, to the rear seat and you had a bed. We really didn't know what do with ourselves, a new, clean car with its own bed. Now that was real cool.

Well, naturally, we had to show off the new car. So like everyone else does, when you want to spread the word, we drove around town. But the real coming out was at the Potter Street picnic.

A new car also meant doing more of what Momma and Grandma loved to do...and that was traveling and fishing. They now had a dependable car, and that also meant, Nola Ruth and I had to do a lot more fishing. Whoppee-do

Now, we really started traveling all over Michigan. We went from Niles to Traverse City, from Monroe to Alpena, to Mackinaw City, to Sault Ste. Marie, back to Lovells, Grayling, Clare and all around Saginaw Bay.

We went to Chicago, Racine and Milwaukee, Wisconsin, and many points in between. Grandma knew people all over the eastern half of the country.

But no city got more visits, planned or on a whim, than Detroit. Grandma's youngest brother, Uncle Alex, lived in Detroit. Uncle Alex lived on St. Aubin Street, right in the heart of Detroit's "Black Bottom."

Occasionally he would move to Chene Street(two blocks away) but he never strayed far from St. Aubin Street. Uncle Alex was very astute and quick witted, although not formally educated. At a time when most everybody didn't know anything about stocks and bonds, he made money on the stock market. That money was part of his safety net when his auto company, Packard Motors, went out of business. He was politically active and racially aware and proud. He personally knew Marcus Garvey, a black activist who was a leader in a movement for blacks going back to Africa and creating their own economic zones of enterprise.

Uncle Alex was an insatiable reader on books of black history and black men. I still have a couple of his books today. He spent many hours talking to me and trying to get me to strive for careers, or business and trades, that would allow me to be my own boss. But I never listened. I ran after the cheese of the corporate world. Years later, after his death or even before he died, I started trying to recall many of his words. I began to read many of his books. I said to myself, if only I had listened, I could be a lot better off...and I'd know a lot more about my history.

## The Jr. Girls

Whatever happened to Octavia? She was so beautiful. The first time that I saw her I fell in love with her. (I was easy in those days)

I met her coming down the basement stairs at the Mason's Lodge Hall in Detroit. Some of us guys were trying to get a jump on the hungry crowd that was about to swarm all over the buffet tables. We were going to sneak into the kitchen and pretend to offer our help. But before turning the corner at the bottom of the stairs, I ran smack into an angel.

Oh, she was not your regular, pretty angel. I could handle those. After all, I was 11 years old, and had dealt with pretty girls before. But this one was different. She was not pretty. She was even beyond being just beautiful. I had never seen anyone like her before.

I staggered backwards, not wanting to touch or soil this object of blinding radiance in front of me.

I stretched out my arms to stop the fellows behind me from crashing into this heavenly being.

### I tried.

I tried to speak, but my throat closed up.

I tried to say excuse me, but only meaningless gurgling came out of my mouth.

I tried to be my normal, suave and debonair self, but I didn't have my smoking jacket.

I tried to tell me, myself, and I that she was only a little girl.

I tried to hide my unsteadiness; this was a new feeling for me.

I tried to pretend that I barely noticed her, but I couldn't stop staring.

I tried to cover up one more blow from those soft, light brown eyes, and I would be down for the count.

I tried to turn away, but I caught a glimpse of a light caramel-colored leg and I felt the free fall of helplessness engulfing me.

I tried, but I wasn't quick enough; I got sucker punched.  I was out cold.

And she knew it.

So there was nothing left for me to do, except act like a little foolish boy, who was in "a whole lot of like!"

How did this happen?  Well one of Momma's special social pleasures was being in the Eastern Star, the female counterpart of the Mason's Lodge.  At one time, she was the leader and trained the Jr. Eastern Stars, the pre-teen girls, on how to march and twirl batons. She wanted to display some of Saginaw's little ones in the annual Detroit parade.

Everyday and Saturday and sometimes twice a day, Momma and other friends would train and practice with the young girls.  They worked on little dance routines and exchanged batons, criss-crossed back and forth, and twirled those batons all the  time.  They were very cute and good too.

So this was the big day.  Momma and her friends were determined to show them, the "citified" Detroiters, what Saginaw girls could do.  The little girls were nervous at first, seeing all the people lining the parade route.  But once they got started, they acted like old troupers.  Everybody thought they were so cute.  They were marching and strutting and twirling, showing off all that stuff that they would have one day.  The "Guiding Light Chapter Jrs." stole the show that year.

After the parade, we all went back to the lodge hall for dinner and grown up talks.  All the boys ran for cover to escape the next boring hours.  Running away, that's how I got blind sided.

I didn't stand a chance with Octavia.  Still I had to try.  She did let me down tenderly.  She was gentle.  I never saw her again.  But I always wondered, "Whatever Happened to Octavia?"

### A golden treasure

Yes, with the new car, Detroit almost became a second home, at least for Momma and Grandma.  One or the other of them was always going to Detroit, but one particular occasion stands out of my mind

One of our most unforgettable Detroit trips happened one day when Momma read in the Detroit Times newspaper that a famous international singing and dancing star was going to be at the Fox

Theatre. She wanted to go and take Nola Ruth and me to see this international star.

So, after quick baths and getting dressed in our Sunday clothes, the three of us along with Grandma piled into the car. We were off to the fabulous Fox Theater in the big "D."

When we arrived at the theater, I remember that it was a cold evening, and we had to park around on the side of the building about a block away. So we were walking fast, huddled over, with our heads bent, leaning into the harsh, biting wind. (OK, so this too isn't part of the '49 summer—please enjoy the snapshot or sue me; no, not that, just call me some names or whatever). We were making our way to the box office, and just as we turned the corner onto Woodward Avenue, we were all startled as we nearly collided with this stunningly, beautiful woman, accompanied by two men in formal attire. Momma, said excuse me, and then looking at the lady, she again said, "Oh, please excuse me."

The beautiful lady replied and said, "That's all right. Nothing happened. If you're going to the show I hope you enjoy it."

Momma was so impressed she said, "She's so nice. Children, that was the star we were coming to see. And one of the white men with her is Buddy Rich, the drummer." I still vividly remember that cold night and looking up into the face of one of the world's most beautiful women, acclaimed and known to the world as Josephine Baker.

For sharing and showing us this moment and many other glimpses of people, life and things, I often told Momma thanks.

## Going Back Down Home

Getting the new car meant Grandma and Uncle Alex both could now take a trip back home to the South, to look up some old relatives. During the years, they had tried to keep up with their relatives. Grandma had sent and received a few cards, but still she had lost touch with most of her people.

Then too, she had always felt that they thought she wanted money or help from them. Grandma had left the South at the age 13 and had had a very rough life. But she had always said that she didn't want anything from the silly fools (those are almost my words, her real

*Uncle Alex and Momma. I should have listened to him more.*

words were more colorful). She and Uncle Alex, just wanted to say hello.

Anyway, when she got her new car, they felt it was good time to go and see where everybody was and how they were doing back home. Yeah, it was a good time to showoff on how well Queen Esther and Alexander had been doing up north.

The main north-south road from Saginaw was US 25. It was a two-lane highway that ran from Michigan to Ohio, Kentucky, Tennessee and Georgia. But the fun part of the route was driving through Kentucky and Tennessee.

Driving around hairpin curves on steep grades, where you lost sight of the road and didn't know which way it turned, was nerve wracking. In the middle of the day the sun blinded you; and at night it was too dark to see. WE WERE SCARED TO DEATH!

Yes driving through Kentucky and Tennessee was very thrilling, if you like the edge of the road in many places to drop off about 200 feet. Also, if you like spots where there were no guardrails, and where there was a guardrail, it was not strong enough to stop a bicycle.

That was my first experience with mountain driving; unfortunately, it was not my last. To this day, I still do not like mountain driving.

We got to Georgia, swung over to Birmingham, Alabama, and Grandma looked up some relatives in Trustville. There she discovered the whereabouts of some relatives in Mississippi.

She was from Mississippi but told people she was from New Orleans. It sounded better. She actually found out about some relatives of Detroit, friends that lived in New Orleans. So the next day we took off for New Orleans, Louisiana.

Driving to Louisiana was a new treat for me. I had never seen Spanish moss before. Spanish moss hanging on the trees gave them an eerie, storybook quality. By this time, the pace of the south, the "take it easy, drift along, it'll get it done, just plain old laid back, way of southern living" was beginning to affect us. We didn't have just the weekend to get our living done. We were taking it a little slower.

The road to New Orleans was gently winding and hilly. It didn't cut through the countryside. It weaved, and unobtrusively, slithered along river banks, and up hills, twisted through valleys, submitted to the dust of the red clay that covered the roots of the yellow pines, which towered above and which at night hid those blacktop pathways, pitching you into real total darkness on moonless nights. There were no street lights or the reflected ambiance of big city lights.

We didn't just look, we took in, the natural, southern differences of nature, as compared to the grandeur of the Great Lakes. We pondered on the destination of the many dirt roads, trails, and pathways that scurried away from the main road.

We fell silent, when at times, while slowly rounding a hill top curve in the road, we would be jarringly yanked back to the reality that made Uncle Alex and many others leave this oasis of genteel, and structured orderly way of life. There, behind those trees or even right at the edge of the road, a building, shack, or lean-to cut into the side of a hill, barely standing, and we saw people.

We were seeing people who were without just about everything. Uncle Alex would say they should come north and get a job. And do better for their families. But we always smiled broadly and waved wildly when one of those families, always a colored family, would be waving and jumping up and down at the joy of seeing some other, "not from around here colored folks" driving a new car. Many did come north.

When we got to New Orleans, we drove through the French Quarter. And once more I was fascinated by the sights and sounds of the story book, French Quarter. We drove around the city. I can only remember that it was different. We found the relatives of the Detroit friends. Uncle Alex knew the Detroiters quite well. We had a nice supper and spent the night on couches and pallets on the floor. The morning breakfast was hot biscuits and butter with sorghum molasses, red-eye gravy, salt cured ham, grits, and some left over red beans and rice. Everything was ate up, and chicory coffee and buttermilk washed it all down.

When we left, they gave us some ham and biscuits to eat on the road. This was just one of the many examples of Southern hospitality that we enjoyed on this trip.

We left New Orleans and headed back to Birmingham. There we found Grandma's first cousin LeRoy Allen. He too had not often replied to her letters. Cousin LeRoy lived in an area of Birmingham called Powderly Hills. He had two children, a son named LeRoy Jr. and a daughter named Ann.

I remember that LeRoy Jr. played the saxophone. Cousin Ann was a teacher. And in their back yard, they had a tree that I had never stolen fruit from, because I had never seen one before, a real live fig tree. The figs were just beginning to ripen. So I ate one, then two, three...and I lost count after that. Then I climbed the fig tree. Those of you who grew up around fig trees know what happened next. I didn't sleep at all that night. I was tossing and turning just a thinking, why did I eat so many figs. But I still like fresh figs. Shortly after that trip, cousin LeRoy moved to Saginaw.

### My second home

After leaving Birmingham, we headed home by way of Fort Wayne, Indiana. There Grandma and Uncle Alex found their eldest half-brother, Ernest. So now I had two uncles named Ernest, one on each side of my family.

Fort Wayne was a town that I liked. I met new guys my age, and maybe it was just because I was there for the summer, but we hit it off real great. I returned to Fort Wayne every summer for at least a month until 1955. There were the Chapman families, Dyke and Hank, cousins, and the rest of their siblings. There was Chuck Lyons, and one of my best summer time buddies, Don Padgett. Every time I hear the song, "Do Nothing Till You Hear From Me," I remember that Don sang that song all summer, so when hearing that song I naturally think of Don. Living in Fort Wayne made me realize that I wanted to leave Saginaw. But after all these years, I still love Saginaw, because it's home.

Good bye old paint. We missed you, but we now realize that your painful sacrifice and death opened up the world to Nola Ruth and I.

Happy trails to the old '36 Dodge, in the summer of '49

## Fishing and Fishing

"Hang on Nola, don't let go of that pole Nola. That must be a big one that you have there," said Clarence, the holiday husband.

"I am holding on. I am not letting go of this fishing pole. He's gonna to have to pull me with him, in order to get away," yelled Grandma.

"Look out Nola, he's heading for those weeds," warned Clarence.

"I see him. He's not going to get over there. I can see what he's trying to do. You look out. Don't slip on those rocks. Where's the net?" Grandma shouted.

"Don't try to lift him out; you'll break the pole. Look out. He's heading back up the river. It's a good thing you got your channel cat line on that pole. Can you see him?" Clarence asked.

"Yeah, yeah, I can make him out. It's getting dark so quick, but I can feel him running. Naw, you ain't going nowhere sucka. Yeah, I gotcha'," she said through grittin' teeth.

That little 4'-10" ball of dynamism was fighting that fish all the way. Straggly sweat-soaked strands of her black Cherokee hair were plastered to her forehead. She was moving up and down the shoreline, stumbling and splashing in and out of the water.

Good Lord, what a monster, she thought. She'd been fightin' this scaly dragon for over ten minutes. He'd already broke off the two foot tip end of the pole. It was just dangling and jerking to every movement of fish and woman. The bamboo cane was showing stress-line strains, like long strings of a rope starting to separate.

Grandma, instead of tiring, seemed to be like plugged into a wall socket and not slowing down at all. In fact it was like she was being recharged at a higher level.

"Here he comes. Where's the net?" she yelled.

"I got it. I see him," exclaimed a wide-eyed Clarence.

Clarence waded into the water and scooped the net along the fish's tail and lifted. Well he tried to lift, but the long net handle started to bend like a wide shaped "u" and then it splintered into so many tooth picks. Clarence re-wrapped the net's drag rope around his arm and with the broken handle again tried to net the fish. This time the fish was not only hooked but finally caught.

"Woo-eh-wee," he half shouted and whistled.

"Look at the size of that. What is it Nola? I ain't never seen one that big. Not up here," marveled Clarence.

"Well I'll be, that's a northern pike. You got to be in deep water normally to catch one those," said Grandma.

Yeah that was Grandma's greatest catch, a 50 inch, 29-1/2 pound northern pike on a cane pole.

Fishing, fishing, and more fishing. That's what the family did best. Grandma and Momma and all of their friends did. And by default, we, Nola Ruth and I, had to fish. To make it clearer, I was doomed to fish and fish.

When you are born into a matriarchal family and the grandmother and mother love to fish—not only for the fun of it, but for the profit of Friday night fish fries—you have little choice but to become a fisherman.

And when you grow up in the Great Lakes State of Michigan, you become very spoiled about seeing large bodies of freshwater, lots of rivers and lakes and bays, like Saginaw Bay, Lake Huron and Lake Michigan. The state of Michigan, which has the longest shoreline of any state in the country, makes you snobbish about the of abundance water and fishing. You're surrounded by Lake Superior, Lake Michigan, Lake Huron, and Lake Erie; and you grow up taking these natural wonders for granted.

It is only when you move into someplace like Las Vegas that you realize that Lake Mead doesn't hold a candle to Lake Huron. But then, you learn to accept Lake Mead for the wonder that it is.

The family did most of their fishing around Saginaw Bay. That area was close enough, about 20 or 50 miles, to go and come back again in a day. These were the days before freeways, and most of the roads were two-lane highways.

There were at least two dozen places that they used to fish around in the Saginaw Bay area. There was Pinconning, where we bought cheese. It was that great tasting sharp cheddar cheese and a variety of other cheeses that I still miss. It was fun just to visit the cheese store.

Then there was the Pine River, especially in the springtime. In the spring, there would be spawning runs of carp fish and a bony fish called a "sucker" and the "red horse," the cousin to the sucker with red fins. You would spear the carp and suckers.

We also fished at Sebewaing, Kawkawlin, and Essexville. But my most favorite place, at least favorite name to say was Quannicassee.

Essexville is the place where Nola Ruth and I liked to go because we played with some kids who lived close by to where we would fish. Every time we came up to fish, they would run over to play with us. Their company was most welcome in the winter, when Grandma and Momma would go ice fishing. Every year we'd meet around the first part of January, and we had lots of fun playing on the ice, while the grown ups fished. I can't remember their names, but it was a boy about my age and a girl about Nola Ruth's age. We just knew that every year, when we went to Essexville, they would show up, and we would play.

### Sanford Dam

You see we have this big swimming pool in Las Vegas, and we don't swim. Oh, we splash around a lot and look cool, but real swimmers we are not.

But and however, I can or have swam. You see it happened this way. Or let's say this is a snapshot of a lifeguard (me) in action.

This actually happened at Sanford Dam in the late spring of 1949. It started when Grandma and Mr. Bob Scott went fishing for rock bass up at Sanford. I did not want to go fishing. Nor did I want to wear a snowsuit. I, all of 11 years old, was too big for snowsuits.

We were fishing just below the dam along the uneven shoreline. There were lots of broken concrete slabs, jutting into the river. At some spots the concrete stuck out into the river about 30 feet.

I picked such a spot, out of the direct sight of Grandma, and naturally at the very edge of a concrete slab. I then proceeded to try and get out of my snowsuit.

I got one strap off one shoulder, and the other strap off the other shoulder. And I was doing great.

Next were the goulashes, those big rubber boots with buckles, in case you didn't know. I pulled them off. Then I got one leg out of the snowsuit and started on the other one.

I really don't know happened to this day. All I know is that I ended up in the water. A long way from shore, and I could not swim. But somehow, I started yelling and kicking because the water was cold.

Then it appeared, as though I was looking at me. I saw me, stroking and stroking and kicking and kicking and making my way towards the shore. I was swimming. Swimming for life itself, mine!

I remember scrapping my knees on the rocks and picking myself up. I looked back, too stunned and cold to feel any emotion. My snowsuit straps were tangled across my shoulder and dripping wet, and it felt like it weighed a ton.

By this time, Grandma and Mr. Bob had come up to me, and once they saw that I was OK, Mr. Bob gave out one of those barrel chested laughs of his and couldn't stop laughing. Grandma, chuckled and then lit into me. She was shouting and wondering what had happened.

Then looking at me again, she said, "So trying to get out of your snowsuit. Serves you right. You should have drowned, scaring folks half to death."

That was the first time I had ever swam, and it was the last time. Every since then all I can do is barely get across the pool. So Sanford Dam has a very special place in my heart.

Every so often, when I go back to Michigan, I drive up there, just to look and see if I can find that spot. But freeways have come through the area and have changed everything.

So although this happened in late spring, it is a part of the summer of '49

I still remember.

## Smelt Dipping

East Tawas and its famous Singing Bridge in the springtime were famed for  the only kind of fishing that I liked.  It was the spring smelt run and smelt dipping.

To go smelt dipping, you arrive at the bridge just about dusk, find a spot, and pitch a little camp because soon there are gonna be hundreds of people around.  You get out your waders and hip boots.  You check your nets.  If you're using cloth mesh nets or galvanized metal nets, you want to make sure that there are no gapping holes.  Next you check the rope and drag bucket or tub you take into the water with you.  Now get your sweatshirts, hoods, coats and gloves, because it was going to get cold.  You'd make a little fire and grill some hot dogs and marshmallows—and wait.

The smelt run normally didn't start until around midnight or one or two o'clock in the morning.  Oh, you'd get one or two smelt coming in all that evening long, but the real run didn't start till late.  At 2 o'clock somebody started running.  Then you'd hear someone yell. "They're running."  Then the whole campsite area would erupt and empty. Guys and gals would be popping up, pulling up waders and hip boots, and pulling on hoods and coats.  They'd start grabbing nets and buckets and start running toward the water.  The shoreline would become a mass of humanity, wading into the little canal coming up from the lake. And the lake would be filled with people, wading out to be the first to start dipping and scooping.

This was the fun part to me.  Wading into the water with that long handle metal net, I'd start scooping and swinging in the water.  Just having a ball, swinging that net through the water.  I could feel the little fishy when they hit the net.  I seldom  got less than a half dozen, maybe a dozen fish.  And I'd turn around to the number two tub or bucket, dump that net full, and turn to scoop some more.

Meanwhile somebody would come out to empty your pail; run

the smelt back to shore, where Momma was preparing a treat.

By this time, the hot dog fire had been converted to a fish fry therapy fire. It was therapeutic because fresh fired smelt straight from the cleanest lake in the world will definitely cure a whole lot of ailments.

That fish fry fire was heating either a big iron pot or skillet, filled with hot grease. Now just take and wash off the sand and loose scales, and that's all the cleaning the smelt got. Next fill a brown paper bag with cornmeal, salt and pepper, paprika and garlic powder, plop in the smelt. Shake well. Then plop those well-seasoned smelt into that hot grease. In about three minutes or five, scoop up a big ladle full. Dump them in a pot with crumpled brown paper, sprinkle with salt; naturally, we never had enough salt, and since we needed more salt, we added more salt. Now grab a little fishey, douse liberally with hot sauce and start eating. And you would end up gingerly blowing and huffing...and flipping that poor little fish from hand to hand because it was hot, stupid! Now you'd grab a piece of light bread and one or two more smelt, lay on more hot sauce, and head back to the lake.

Dipping again, scooping again, dumping your bucket again. I didn't mind this kind of fishing because, you did not have to wait forever for something to bite. Here it was dip and dump. In about an hour's time, we'd fill one number two tub to the top with smelt. But naturally we never went to get just one number two tub. We always took two and sometimes three.

Yes, I enjoyed the dipping and eating fried smelt at the shoreline, outdoors under the stars, and yes, the people. People came from all over the Midwest, laughing and drinking Kool-Aid and beer and having a good time.

One year we meet a grocery store owner who had a store just down the street from our Uncle Ernest in Fort Wayne, Indiana. He was doing the same thing we were doing; dipping smelt and selling them back home.

Now the real fun began. It is one thing to cook and eat the smelt "au naturale" or as they come from the water; however, you can't sell them that way to all people. Therefore, once you get the smelt home, you'd really have to clean them, one by one. That's the part I did not like. Nola Ruth didn't like it either.

Once we got home, we'd put some ice chips and blocks of ice in some water in the bathtub, and start cleaning and cutting the fishes.

*Uncle Ernest Hayes, Grandma's lost brother we found in Ft. Wayne, Indiana. He is between the ages of 30 and 40 years old in this picture. That means it would have been taken in the mid twenties or early thirties.*

A number two tub can hold hundreds of smelt. It took nearly half a day to clean all the smelt. And that was with three or four adults and two very slow kids.

Sometimes you'd popped little heads and pull out the entrails, which was the easiest way to do it; or else, you would slit them open and go to it. Then we would wrap them in freezing paper and put them in the freezer. We would have a lot of smelt. But over the next couple of months between our Friday night fish fries, Saturday night rent parties, and just plain party partyies, at least 90 per cent of them would be gone. The rest the family would enjoy during the rest of the year.

## Back to Straight Fishing

"You've got a bite Mickey. You're bobber is moving."

That's a little floating device on the line that lets you know if fishes are fighting over the bait that I didn't have on my hook.

"Pick up your pole," said Grandma. "You got something on your line."

"Hurry up and do somehing boy," Grandma would be yelling by now.

I would run over to the pole and yank it so hard that the hook would fly out of the fish's mouth. Don't yank so hard, set the hook first. Then pull him out, everybody would say.

Then Grandma would say let me get there. You don't want to fish anyway.

"Get out the way boy," she'd say.

And that was OK with me, because now I could find another spot, farther away from Grandma and look for more rocks and arrow heads. I could also watch the little minnows or fish in the water at the bank

In the normal course of events, a fishing trip involved tying perhaps a half dozen bamboo cane poles on top of the car and taking off. Poles were of all sizes, varying in range from 4 to 12 feet. Most of them were around 8 or 10 feet for the grown ups. The kids, who did not want to fish anyway, normally only dealt with six-foot poles.

We used fishing poles simply because they were cheaper than

rods and reels. We knew about rods and reels, but they cost real money, more than we wanted to spend. Thus we had fishing poles on top of the car.

Once you got to your fishing hole, you'd untie the poles from the top of the car, and unwrap them from the blankets or sheets that were wrapped around the hooks and sinkers. Next, start untangling lines and hooks, and bait the hooks.

Now your job was to find that special spot, along the shore, where you expected to catch the most fish. You have to be very critical. The spot had to have a good standing or sitting area, with not too many weeds or rocks to get your line hung up on. You also had to look out for low hanging tree branches. Next, you had to be far enough away from everyone else to keep your lines from getting tangled up with others. For the kids, that meant finding a spot that Grandma and Momma approved.

Then bait your hook and throw out your pole, oops, I mean line and wait for the fish that would never bite your hook, because you had learned how to make the bait come off once the hook was in the water. So now I could wander around looking for something else to do.

Of course on this day at Edenville, things did not follow the script. By the time, I was into some serious rock throwing and diligent arrowhead hunting, I only found two in over ten years of avoiding fishing.

After awhile Momma and Grandma would check on me to see what I was doing and make me put bait on the hook, so it didn't fall off.

After about an hour, we would pack up all the all the poles again and move around to another spot or the other side of the river. This would go on until we found the right spot, where the fish were buying the rights to bite on our hook. After four to about six hours, we normally had a good mess of fish, and it would be time to go home.

This should have been mentioned earlier, but before you go fishing, you had to have bait. Our main bait was earthworms, little bitty ones, and the big fat night crawlers. You had to dig for worms, and I did more digging than me wanted to. But to get night crawlers, you used a shocking rod. You made one by getting a long iron or steel rod, tape a wooden handle onto it, then attach some bare electric wires to it and plug the other end of what was usually a lamp cord into an outlet. Push the rod deep into some good wet ground and wait for the night crawlers to start popping up. You'd then take a flashlight and start picking up the prize. The night crawlers were kept in a worm farm that the family made.

Since we went fishing so much, we had to take good care of them. And it was Mickey's job to keep the worm farm clean. I was not the best worm keeper. Nola Ruth was worst; she would pull a worm apart and put the pieces back in the bin and soon all the worms would be dead.

Such as it was in the summer of '49.

I still remember.

## The Long Fishing Trip

Two or three times every summer, Grandma and Momma would take an extended fishing trip across the state. We would start out in Saginaw and go to Muskegon. Grandma's favorite fishing spot in Muskegon was right in the middle of Mona Lake Bridge. She wasn't fishing for just any kind of fish or for any fish to bite on the hook. No, she was fishing specifically for big beautiful silver bass and lots of them. In those years, Muskegon was a place to catch silver bass.

On these trips, we would normally spend the day fishing and the night at the homes of friends or in the car and tents.

I used to love these trips, because like Grandma, I loved to travel. Nola Ruth never liked to travel. She got car sick. However, once we made her go someplace, she had more fun than anyone else. Momma also loved to travel. Love of travel was a family birth mark.

But Momma couldn't travel as much as she wanted, because she had to look after the property and pickup the loose ends when Grandma dropped the ball. Grandma really didn't care about details. So of course, she was always dropping the ball.

But since Momma had been foolish enough to learn how to drive, she was now present on a lot more of the long trips.

On the trips, we never got to see too much of any town because we were always heading for the nearest fishing spot. So the only thing I can remember about Muskegon is how good the silver bass tasted and the fact that we always caught plenty of them.

After leaving Muskegon, we headed for Baldwin and Idlewild. Michigan was kind of a funny state in that you never knew where you would find black folks living. And Grandma could find people in some of the most faraway and out of the way places.

In these small towns, over here or there was always one-person, one family or two, who lived there. This fact is most striking when I think of all the times our family went to Baldwin. Imagine my surprise when years later I learned that that town had been a childhood home to one of America's greatest actors, James Earl Jones. If you grew up in Michigan around '49 in a town or area where there were so very few Negroes, each new encounter with another Negro was always acknowledged, at least by a nod or some subtle gesture.

When you discover any small common thread, that you have with someone, be they famous or not, you also at the same time acquire a small sense of kinship. I didn't know any body in Baldwin, Michigan, but Grandma knew people in Baldwin.

So we would fish during the day and spend the night with friends. For example, Mr. Shorty (that's Mr. Big Shorty; Mr. Little Shorty lived 'round Sanford Dam) lived just outside of Baldwin. To get to his place, you go on past the old boarded up gas station. After about a mile, there's a sandy road, kitty-corner off to your left that you take. Now, she thinks you turn right at the second cross road and look for a yellow school house, after 'bout two or three miles, and turn on the first road with a name sign on it...it should be Black River Creek Road...make another right. Then look for his driveway, about two miles. She can't remember his house or lot number. He's suppose to have a big red and yellow barrel by the drive. Then once you see the barrel turn right, (the only way you can turn) and drive on back to the house. Well, we looked and looked, for that barrel and never did find it. Just as we were giving up, Nola Ruth said, "there's two little cute red and yellow buckets next to those people's driveway."

At that Grandma said, "back up Lois, that looks like it could be the place." And it was. Fortunate for us, that little sister wasn't looking for the barrel. She was just day dreaming and looking out the window.

Like I said, you'd never expect to find black folks in the country, out from the many small villages and settlements in Michigan. However, if any lived there, chances were nine out of ten that Grandma knew them or how to get to their place

## *Idlewild*

The next morning we would normally be off to go fishing somewhere else. However, this morning we were on our way to Idlewild which is only a hop, skip, and a jump from Baldwin. Idlewild, Michigan, was the playground for all classes of Negro America in the forties and fifties. It was recognized as a total family playground throughout the Midwest. Some people came from New York, New England, and, as far west as St. Louis and Kansas City.

There were country stores, vacation cabins and empty lots, fishing streams and lakes, sandy beaches for swimming, boating ramps, canoes, and one or two good restaurants. There were small bars and clubs. But the crown jewel of clubs in Idlewild was the El Morocco Show Bar. It was owned by Arthur Braggs from Saginaw, Michigan. The club provided first-rate, top of the line entertainment.

Mr. Braggs and Grandma were good speaking and drinking acquaintances. They both were in the business of providing entertainment to the public.

Mrs. Braggs was on the nursing Board at Mt. Olive Baptist Church. She and Momma were on good terms. Both she and Momma, each in their own way, lived in two different and separate worlds than the one that was around them. One world was providing entertainment to the world. The other world was seeking salvation for the world and themselves. A strange paradox that many people still fight today.

Entertainers, who came to Idlewild in the forties and fifties are legend:

There was Arthur Prysock and his brother Red;

There was Louis Jordan and his tymphony five;

There was Duke Ellington and his big band;

There was  the bandleader Count Basie;

There was blues singer, Ivory Joe Hunter;

There was the silky piano styling and the gravelly velvet voice of Nat King Cole

And later, the song styling of Della Reese.

Yes, the El Morocco Show Bar's entertainment was the equal of any top-flight nightclub in the country. And its setting, next to a beautiful lake with little cottages and cabins all-around in the middle of a pine forest, was breath taking

But Idlewild fell victim to the same curse that slowly squeezed out the life of Negro Major League baseball—integration.

Whereas, integration was necessary in order for America to survive, it seemed that the greatest price for integration was paid by black enterprises of the fifties. These enterprises no longer had a captive audience or a dedicated clientele, and white America didn't even know about, care about, and would not support them.

So hid from the sunlight of inclusion and choked off from the breath of new markets, they were slowly entwined by isolation and left gasping for life, buffeted and ignored in a crowded train station of growth and prosperity.

Thus chained with a dwindling, aging, and scattered customer base, these businesses died on the vines of social and economic progress, just as micro-economic lives are sacrificed today for the good of economic globalization.

Now that we were in Idlewild, our first order of business was to find a camping spot somewhere in the El Morocco parking lot that could be watched by the attendants. You see, the Nash had a bed; and Nola Ruth and I slept in our tent.

We loved that tent. I had my Boy Scout flashlight, and Nola Ruth had her brownie flashlight. We would pretend to pass signals back for and forth, giggling and laughing all night long or least until I fell asleep. Naturally Grandma and Momma would have the parking lot guys looking out for us, but bad things just didn't hardly ever happen to kids in those days.

Meanwhile Momma and Grandma would be having a good time; listening to a new blues song, or whatever, dancing, and rubbing elbows with the black stars and celebrities of the moment. This networking was also good business for Momma and Grandma.

Why? Because black entertainers could not stay at white hotels, even in Michigan in the forties and fifties. So when traveling to small towns, that meant the entertainers stayed with the promoters who booked them, and/or stayed at rooming and boarding houses of people in the community. And since Grandma knew Mr. Braggs and others, every now and then when there was a shortage of rooms, Grandma would always be glad to help out.

Let me tell you about our most famous overnight visitor. It happened this way. There was a big dance at the Saginaw auditorium, and the main headliner did not show up. So, the promoter offered a refund to anyone, who didn't want stay and see the second act. Well Momma and Aunt Lillian were determined to have a good time that evening; so they stayed to see this new piano player with a drummer and guitar player. After the show, the entertainers needed some place to sleep. So naturally, Momma offered her hospitality. When they arrived back home, Momma and Aunt Lillian fried up some chicken, fish, and french fries; and I think she said they had some leftover greens and cole slaw. So they all ate and started another party, and that piano player played on our out of tune piano until the sun came up. They had a great time. Shortly, after leaving Saginaw that piano player released a song that catapulted him to the top of the entertainment world. The name of the song was get your kicks on "Route 66." The name of the entertainer was a man called Nat King Cole

Meanwhile, back in the tent, Nola Ruth and I were trying to read comic books by our flashlights, but the batteries were getting weak. This was a long time before the pink bunny came along. So there was nothing else to do, but tell ghost stories and go to sleep.

But morning again, it came too soon. Yes, like always, it was bright and too early. Next came the shaking and beating on the tent, trying to wake us up; or least trying to wake me up. Now I wake up slow and in a quiet mood. Forget that others say I'm grouchy. I say quiet and meditative. Nola Ruth, on the other hand, wakes up being so mean and evil, that it's a good thing she didn't make herself. I mean low down, absolutely mean and evil (just for the record she got pay back, her daughter is the same way). And on that cool, crisp, northern Michigan morning, things were no different. I was contemplative; Nola Ruth was just mean and evil.

Grandma was saying, "Get up you kids. The fish are biting. Let's go. We're going to go on the other side of the lake this morning. That appears to be where they're catching the most fish, and we didn't come all this way to go back home with nothing."

"Mickey, you had better get yourself together," said Grandma.

"And Nola Ruth, stop rolling your eyes and go wash up."

Well, we spent the day driving and fishing all around the lake and up and down a few rivers. When we returned to the club, we packed the fish in fresh ice and asked Mr. Braggs for use of one his freezers. Then we went to our camping spot and opened up our unique, Western Auto Store picnic table and seats that folded up like a suitcase. It is not so unique today, but it was almost twenty years before Sears started selling them. We had hot dogs and burnt marshmallows. Momma would play some games with us, and we'd walk around the woods, just a little bit. Then, before you knew it, the sun was not only going down, but almost gone. So back to the parking lot camp site and sleep for us kids and party time for Momma and Grandma.

After leaving Idlewild, we headed north to Cadillac to fish around there for a little while. Then east, across the state, past Houghton and Higgins lakes, on our way to Mackinaw City. This part of the trip took most of the day. Once we arrived, Grandma had to look up a guy named Sam, who was an important clog in this long fishing trip.

Sam was a general caretaker and handyman for many absentee owners, who had cottages and cabins in the area. And he always knew whose cabin was available, on what weekend or what days. Therefore, we were able use a cabin, and cleanup after our stay, leaving it in better shape than when we came in. Sam got profuse praise on how well and clean he kept the cottage, and we had a nice place to spend the night. Everybody was happy.

Thirteen years later I spent my honeymoon in Mackinaw City, and I found Sam and reminded him of the many times he helped our family. It felt good finding Sam and showing him that I was grown up and was trying to "amount to somethin'."

Around this area of the state you caught a lot of Sunfish, Bluegills, Crappies and Rock Bass. That's why Momma and Grandma came to fish in this area. They were not disappointed. They caught more fish, enough now to fill a second cooler. We all ready had more fish than I wanted to clean, and they were still going for more.

On this particular trip, most of the first day in Mackinaw City, was spent finding Sam and then fishing. On the second day, Grandma wanted us to relive a part of her history. We got up early that day and took the ferry (this was before the bridge was built) across the Straits of Mackinac to St. Ignace. From there we drove up to the Sault Locks, at Sault Ste. Marie, Michigan. There, Grandma found the old house, that she had owned and ran as a boarding house during the 1920s around '29, when the locks were being worked on. Grandma was always trying to make an independent buck, one way or another. The house was occupied by Chippewa Indians. Grandma introduced herself and pointed out that once she had lived in the house.

After returning across the Straits to go home, we took the scenic route of US 23, around Lake Huron on our way back to Saginaw. Stopping to do little fishing at Singing Bridge in East Tawas. When we got around to the Saginaw Bay area, we bought some country honey, lots of cheese, and some sausage in Pinconning. By the time we got home, it was dark and very late; and we all were very tired. We had caught a lot of fish, two coolers, just full of fish. We filled half the bath tub with ice, dumped the fish into the bath tub, and then filled the tub with more ice and went to bed.

And when the morning comes, there would be a lot of work to do. And the morning came. Then the only business of the day was scaling and gutting and cleaning fish. Afterwards, it would take weeks to rid the kitchen of all the fish scales.

With so much fish, scaled, cleaned and ready to cook, guess what the weekend special was going to be. Yes sirree, bop, fish sandwiches, french fries and cole slaw, and did I say, fish dinners, fish sandwiches, fish snacks, fish, fish and more fish. And to tell the truth, a fish sandwich laced with plenty of hot sauce, some hot, salty and brown paper bag greased drained french fries, washed down with a bottle of smooth, cold, refreshing Champagne Velvet beer, was very good eating and drinking.

Chomping and chewing on a spicy hot fish sandwich wrapped in newspaper (when we ran out of wax paper) was and still is good eating—especially while waiting for a chair to open up at the coon-can or tonk table or listenin' to some low down dirty blues on our multi-colored juke box.

On these extended fishing trips around the state, Nola Ruth and I were always amazed that Grandma knew somebody, just about everywhere we went. Grandma knew a lot of people all over the country. I'll tell you that part of her story in another story one day.

As far as this story goes, the long fishing trips meant traveling, and seeing different things and I loved it. It was going to other parts of the state or other states that shined a light on how much world there was outside of the Saginaw island.

The trips were part of having fun in the summer of '49.


I still remember.

# BAY CITY HIGHWAY PICNIC

*Get Ready 'Cause Here We <u>ALL</u> Come*

Walter rolled out of bed. How did he get into this mess? He had had a rough night. He was tired and still sleepy and wondered why he volunteered to be one of the crew to set up the picnic area? But he knew that he was always one of the first to volunteer. He turned and looked at his wife, still asleep in bed, and got up slowly, hoping not to awaken her.

He walked over to the dresser to shut off the alarm clock, before it had a chance to go off. He then went into the bathroom to wash up and so on. Afterwards he put on some blue jeans, an undershirt and a regular shirt. By this time, his wife was awake and sitting up in bed. She was reaching for her bathrobe and slippers and asked him if he wanted a cup of coffee or breakfast before he left.

Walter said that he would like a thermos of coffee to take with him, and one or two sandwiches. He would be back to pick her up and take the rest of the their things to the picnic.

Walter also had to pick up Louis and George and meet some of the other guys at the picnic spot on Bay City highway. They were planning to get to the Veterans Memorial Pavilion before daybreak to secure and clean the picnic area.

## *The Setting*

The Bay City highway was a four-lane road approximately 13 miles long, running from Saginaw, north to Bay City. The highway started in Saginaw by the Gray Iron foundry, winding past the slag heaps and sludge dumps and across railroad tracks, past the muskrat farms, and onwards to the other "city by the bay."

It was a winding road that followed the Saginaw River, with large green areas, particularly on the river or west side of the road. Like most highways in those days, where there were nice roadside green spots with trees around, you could, normally, find a picnic table and a small grill. Families and friends during the week, and on weekends, would drive out to these highway, vacation spots for picnics and cook outs.

Along the Bay City highway, there were many such spots on both sides of the road. The nicest area was about eight miles north of town. It was the Veterans Memorial Building. There you had rest rooms, a pavilion, and an activity center.

## *The Birth Of The Picnic*

The picnic started out being limited to several church summer Bible school's programs. It was a churches only picnic. And you know church and street people don't mix publicly. But with the kids from large and small churches, store front churches, basement churches and tent churches, you needed a lot of adult supervision.

So, by the time you got all the adults needed to help monitor and control the children, you had quite a crowd already. And some of the adults, in turn, invited their friends to join them, because they wanted someone to talk to besides just kids all day long.

When you extend invitations like that, you get a lot of people in a short time, all kinds of people. And the church folk were real upset that street and sporting life people would be at the picnic. You see those folks don't publicly do things together. In fact there was talk of calling it off because there would be more street folks than church folks. But the cat was out of the bag, and this thing had seemed take on a life of its own and the churches had to go through with it.

Besides, every one was good at heart and just wanted the kids to have some, good clean fun.  So people from all levels of society came together eager and ready to help out the kids

Therefore the self righteous Eastsiders and their friends, for that day, unturned their noses at Miss So and So; ignored the fact that Mr. Brainy Boy was a social entrepreneur, or as my sister would have me say it, he lived the "sporting life." (Does that phrase, mean anything to anyone under 45?)  Really, it was all about letting the kids have fun.

You see everybody was somebody's aunt, uncle, cousin, step-father, Grandma, or grandpa.  We were all related, some way or another; and for once, the kids could openly enjoy being and playing with all their relatives, even the sisters and bothers that they weren't supposed to know about.  Yeah this was the picnic of all picnics that summer.

So, it was at Mt. Olive, Tabernacle, Bethel, and a lot of other churches (and I don't remember the names of them all) that this idea got this started.  And like mushrooms, in dark room or Nola Ruth repeating the tales, she heard when hiding under the front porch, listening to grown up gossip, the picnic just grew, and...

**the word spread:**
- The Word Spread to the families on Myrtle Street,
- to the Garretts and quiet ones of Dywhite Street,
- all up-and-down Farewell Street, to First Street, and the Tuckers, Sanders, and Perkins;
- to the notorious 7th Street gang, the Ruffins, Washingtons, Pattons, Moores, and Masons;
- then to both of the Scott families, and that was a lot of folks;
- then to the Halls, and there were a million Halls.

**the word spread**
- to the friends of the family
    Miss Bernice and her son, Ollie
    Miss Cooper and little Joyce
    Miss Cripple Hattie and her son Theodore
    Miss Polly, her mother and son, Jitterbug
    to around the corner to our friend from Panamá, Mrs. McLean
    our next-door neighbors, the McGee's, and their relatives,
    and there were a lot of them too.

**the word spread**
- down and up, all of the First Ward,
- then the word crossed the tracks,
- to the Jones, the Farrells, the Browns, the Bonds, the Williams,
- to the Sparks, the Stevens, and on and on

**the word spread to**
- the south side of town,
  the Allens, the McClains and the Boyds,
  to Lee Otis, and my second grade, second or third love,
  his sister, Irma Lee
  the quiet Caseys
  all from Salina grade school

**the word spread**
- way out to the country,
  to 23rd Street, and Outer Drive and Indiantown

In fact, it was all over town that the people of color, and their friends, which later came to mean the "Eastiders and Their Friends," were having a community picnic.

**Yes The Word Spread !**

So Walter's wife prepared his coffee and made his pressed ham sandwiches. Meanwhile, Walter got some shovels, rakes, and brooms out of the garage, and put them in the car.

The car pulled itself out of the driveway, and it drove to George's house. At George's house, Walter, now a part of the conscious world, pulled into the driveway and softly blew his horn. George was ready, and in his easy long strides, walked down the long side porch of his home. He turned and waved goodbye to his wife and oldest son, who was standing by the door, and got in the car with Walter.

When they got to Louis' house, he was sitting on the front steps, waiting for them. Each had a thermos of coffee and a bag of sandwiches. So off they went to their spot along the highway of life.

In the years before and since that day, quite a few lives were started, somewhere along that highway.

Walter with his eight or nine other buddies staked out about 10 picnic tables, and at least a half dozen grills around the Pavilion.

When finished with that, they looked up. The sun was just

beginning to peek over the tops of the trees and the streaks of red and yellow sunlight, filtering through the maple and oak leaves, were being pierced by the needles of the tall, evergreen pine trees.

The dew of the night, had softened the crunch of the evergreen's bed of brown needles. And the dew, on the grass, left summer ski trails where the first steps of Walter's trail blazers splattered the jeweled droplets of moisture. The morning birds sang out in praise for the new day, and I suspect, some protested at being disturbed.

They all poured a cup of coffee, lit a cigarette, took a deep breath, looked at the rising sun of the dawn, and smiled big broad smiles. Yes, they all felt like it was going to be a nice day for the picnic.

Next, they started raking up dead leaves and grass and other debris. All the papers, trash, pop and beer bottles were put in barrels and kroger sacks and burlap bags. The most unpleasant job was cleaning the restrooms. More correctly, the out door toilets had to be made usable and breathable. The latter task required the dumping of several bags of lime down those little holes.

By this time, some other men and teenagers had arrived. So now, the teens could clean the tables. The tables were dirty, stained with mustard and ketchup, and were the recipients of the blessing from above, in the form of droppings from birds.

The tables were made of logs and were heavy. It took, at least, six teens to carry one table. Thus the table and water bucket brigade lines were formed. You could not just dump buckets of water on the tables at the Pavilion, because the area would become muddy and slippery. So you had to take the tables to the river water.

Let it be said, some of the boys didn't have to, but wanted to, "Wade In The Water," just like that old gospel song. Unfortunately, the experience did not "save" their souls, but they had fun.

So with lines of water-filled, splashing buckets, and armed with bars and bars of Fels-Napta Soap and scrub brushes, the tables and outhouses were made clean enough to pass Grandma's inspection.

Next they cleaned the grills. By this time, hot dogs, ring bologna, ribs and chicken, had been delivered to the site in number two wash tubs, filled with ice. Along with the number two wash tubs, filled with ice, there were two trucks, each, with three ice boxes for perishable foods. So as each family arrived, they took their salads and meats to the Pavilion. In the back, bags of charcoal were piled up, waiting for the hot and sizzling role they had that day.

'Round about this time, Mr. Shorty, from Sanford, arrived with his truck. He had welded two sets of three, number two tubs together, and he hauled them around in the back of his truck. So when Mr. Shorty and that truck showed up, it was a big party going on, and people were about to get down to some real serious barbecueing.

## Tires Ain't What They Used To Be

"Hey Walt, we'd better get back and pick up the old lady and the kids," George yelled out from the ball field.

Some of the guys, who arrived early like Walt and them, had already gone back home, to pick up their families. So Walter and his crew started back to town and just as they crossed the railroad tracks, after the big curve that merged into Washington Street, they had a flat tire, and they didn't have a spare tire.

Tires and inner tubes were not as reliable in those days, as they are today. And for the most part, you did your own patchin' and repairin'. After taking out the shovels and rakes in the trunk, they found the jack and got the flat tire off the car. They were going to patch it there but decided to roll it down to the 10th Street gas station, about five or four or five blocks away and see if somebody they knew was workin' and would fix it for next to nothin' or less.

When they got there, Otis, Louis' cousin, was working and when he saw them, he started laughin' and signifin'.

"Y'all, know better than to be ridin' more than two blocks in Walter's car. You know with his tires he cain't run over a piece of chalk, let alone cross railroad tracks. I been trying to get my cheap buddy to at least buy some good used tires, 'cause I know buying anything new is out the question with him," said Otis...and he was just getting started.

While waiting for Otis, to finish patchin' the tire, they had a couple bottles of the best grape pop ever made, "O-So-Grape." Otis let Walter and George use his car to go back to Walter's car.

Louis, stayed at the station, where he and Otis, continued to swap lies. As the old saying goes, the first lie doesn't stand a chance. The second one is always bigger. By the time Walt and the others got home, the wives were not in the best of moods.

It was now about eight o'clock. People and families were beginning to arrive and started staking claims to their little spots. By now, there were close to 100 people present, taking up about a quarter-mile stretch along the highway. It was quite a show for other highway travelers. People kept arriving and leaving and coming back all day long.

Immediately, after the cars were unloaded, tables were covered with old tablecloths or old sheets. Contributions to the community pot luck were taken to the Pavilion, and volunteer workers were checking in. And the kids were hungry.

There were egg sandwiches, tin cans for cereal, peanut butter and jelly sandwiches, and salami sandwiches.

However, serious breakfast eatin' people had brought pots and skillets, and they had in their procession slabs of bacon, sausage, half a ham, or/and, pork chops with the intent to scrambled eggs, prepare grits, and/or fry onions and potatoes.

And on top of that, they were going to make cold water corn bread cakes, or skillet quick biscuits or flat bread, and then spread and smothered it all in butter and some down home, Ala-Ga syrup or molasses.

These people not only created envy; naw, they made everybody mad. Because they couldn't quietly eat, their little, all right, big breakfast. They had to tease and joke about how good their breakfast was. I tell you they threatened the restraint of us all. But you had to admit they were some serious breakfast eaters.

After breakfast, the kids wanted to play, and about 47 minutes later, they were hungry again and wanted hot dogs, candy, cake, cookies, kool-aid, burnt marshmallows, any kind of sandwich, and of course, hot dogs.

The Mother Board members of the various churches were in charge of cooking and organizing the food arrangements. The term "Bar b que, grilling" had not been invented; and therefore, cooking, or making bar b que, was not a male dominated, "show off" activity. Queing, was a shared activity.

By now, the number two wash tubs, charcoal fires were ready, and the ribs and chicken were being initiated into the world of barbecue.

Or as my sister would have me say, they started cookin' the meat.

Back at the individual tables and grills, hot dogs, burnt marshmallows, and, sausages were being devoured. So it was time for the fun and games to begin.

### Did You Catch Any?

Where there's water, there is fish. Where there is fish, Grandma is gonna try and catch them (even in the not too clean Saginaw River). But she was not alone. There were other real serious fishermen among us.

They came with cane poles tied atop the cars. They moved away from the crowd, up the river a ways, to see if anything was biting. And some were catching a couple of small carp, and one guy had a string of about half a dozen bullheads. But Grandma wasn't having any luck today.

She was using her favored fishing pole, the ten footer. So far, the fish were having more fun than she was. They were eating more than she was too, her bait.

She eventually ran out of worms, and guess who was walking by me. She saw me, so I had to run back to the car to get some worms. Well, I got the worms, but Grandma's luck didn't change.

Meanwhile, the young teens and Mr. Rodger had a softball game going on at the Pavilion playing field. It was the boys against the girls. And boys were not doing very well. But then, the girls were not doing well either. Everybody was just getting dusty, dirty and having a ball (pun intended, that is if there is one).

Having just as much fun at another field, the smaller kids were playing mixed team softball. And the real young kids—the preschoolers, kindergartners and first-graders—were playing hide and seek among the pine trees and bushes.

Fingers, Lionel, Joe, and Butter were catching fly balls being hit by Mr. George. Some other guys were playing touch below the belt football, and some were playing basketball. And everybody who wanted to—young or old, male or female—were playing volleyball.

A group of older teens, boys and girls, were just walking along the river, teasing each other about who liked who; who was going with who; and who was cheatin' on who. Oh, they were also talking about high school, and what they were going to do after they graduated. Girls were trying not to spend too much time or show too much caring towards any one boy, because the last thing they wanted was for momma or daddy to become suspicious about anyone they could put a name to.

Somewhere in the distance, across the fields, big and little boys were calling out for hot dogs, smoked sausages, ring bologna, pickle loaf sandwiches, water melon, and just plain old "some thin' to eat," and did I say hot dogs.

We were blessed that day. The angels smiled down upon us, because for all the eating that went on that day, they did not run out of hot dogs.

## The Chow Down

Eventually you had to get down to the main activity of the day. The second most important reason for this gathering, the EATING! It was getting on time to start the big "Chow Down." By now, the ribs and chicken were coming off the tubs and grills at a smooth and steady rate, that was increasingly faster.

Pans were being filled with slabs of ribs and chickens, that after being mopped with lemony basting sauce and then being mopped with the final hot or mild real bar-b-que sauce, the "Meat" was again slowly cooked over the ash-coated charcoal embers.

It was so that the twang of the tenderizing, lemon's flavor would gently pull at your cheeks.

It was so that the honey or brown sugar and tomatoes deepened the red glow of the sauce that glazed the slabs.

It was so that the pungency of the garlic and onion pierced the surface of the meat and fat to the bone and grisle.

It was so that the subtlety of all the spices and flavors could be given their just expression.

So after being be baptized and sanctified with the sauce of truthfulness, these ribs pointed the way to gastronomic salvation.

It was so because these bones were seared and sealed by the fires of purity on those famous "Number Two Wash Tubs."

Or as my sister would have me say, when the meat was done, they put it in some pans so people could eat.

The ladies were setting up the tables, and all of the pot luck bounty was beginning to fill the tables:

- There were string beans, and string beans with potatoes, and string beans with carrots, potatoes and okra.
- There were mustard greens, turnip greens and smothered cabbage. It was too early for collard greens, but still there were some collard greens.
- Naturally, all green beans, greens and cabbage dishes were cooked with salt pork, jowl bacon, ham, ham bones, smoke neck bones or/and ham hocks (so much so and so concern 'bout cholesterol and high blood pressure. You was gonna die of somethin' anyway).
- There were carrot casseroles, corn casseroles, turnip and rutabaga dishes, and mashed potatoes and all kinds of gravy.
- There were baked beans, red beans and rice, navy beans and, pinto beans, butter beans, great northern beans and kidney beans.
- And all were cooked with the standard seasoning meats.
- We had corn on the cob, fried corn and roasted corn.
- There was Momma's version of succotash, corn, tomatoes, celery, onions and okra.
- There were three or four kinds of macaroni and cheese. Everyone had their own version of that dish.
- There was cole slaw, potato salad, macaroni salad, tomatoes, onions and cucumbers, and a half a dozen kinds of fruit salads.
- There was a fruit table filled with watermelon, cantaloupe, honeydew melons musk melons blackberries, cherries, grapes, plums and did I say watermelon
- There were biscuits, homemade loaves of breads, homemade rolls, corn bread and hot and cold water corn bread flat cakes.
- There was the meat, other than main course, of barbecue ribs and chicken.
- We had fried chicken, barbecued neck bones, pig feet and goat, baked lamb breast and shoulder.
- Then there was, smoked ham, roasted fresh ham, baked chicken and cornbread dressing, baked coon and sweet potatoes.
- Somebody brought a big pot of pig feet and knuckles, cooked

in a tomato and onion sauce.
- Then there were the goodies tables, the tables for desserts.
- There were apple pies and loads of sweet potato pies.
- There were all kinds of cakes.  Momma made her six layer Kool-Aid cake.
- The tables were covered with, chocolate cakes, yellow cakes, caramel cakes, spice cakes, coconut cakes, and lemon cakes. Almost all of the cakes were at least three layers high, and some were four layers high.  People just believed that a special cake had to be a big cake.
- And then there were the cobblers: the peach, the apple, the cherry, and the blackberry.  Oh, don't let me forget, the peach cobblers.
- There were oatmeal cookies filled with chocolate chips, date bars, brownies fudge bars and so on.

Everyone donated their best dishes.  There was lots of every thing. All of the Pavilion tables were filled, and we still needed more tables. Food, fun, games and friendship were the order of the day.

### Show Me Your Love

It was amazing to see how the love of, and for, the children gave witness to the adage that a child will lead them.  For without the love of everyone for their own children, and the caring for all the of the community's children, then this display of the bountiful, generous, and warm-over flowing of food would have not been possible.

The feeling that enveloped everyone, that sense of family and that awareness of us all being in the same family, gave proof to the strength of the love that was felt for our children.  For a few hours, all of the community—saint, sinners and everyday people—actually lived like we loved each other every day.  Yes, it is amazing what the kids can do for us.

### Let's eat

"Hey y'all.  Stop playing and come on over here.  The ministers are gonna bless the food," as Mother Boyd was trying to get everybody together.

"You children quit playin' and get on over here," called out Mother Harper.

If seemed like it took about another five or ten minutes to get all those people settled down. But whatever it was now after noon, before long, it'd be closer to one o'clock. With everybody gathered 'round, all the ministers joined together in a common prayer.

The blessings were no sooner finished than everybody started yellin' "let's eat."

So the lines formed, with very little pushing and shoving. and the people began to fill their plates.

Someone said, "Give me some of that macaroni and cheese. I didn't know you could make it that way."

"Momma, I want some of your potato salad, and your fried sweet potatoes," someone else called out.

"Those greens sure look good, and I see that some body's cooking collards, before the first frost."

Someone would say, "I didn't know you could make macaroni salad; this is good."

Someone else said, "I never mixed cabbage with my greens before; it's not too bad."

"What about that chicken, Gloria? Don't forget to get me some fried chicken and that fresh ham. I want to try that," says Mother Bell.

The old folks didn't have to stand in line, one of their relatives or friends would always take care of them.

Food on the tables was being consumed at the speed of chompin' teeth and lickin' fingers. And just as fast as a dish or pan was emptied, it was replaced with heaping full ones of more good whatever. Side dishes, vegetables, salads and breads were being consumed as quickly as the meat dishes.

Somebody was complaining that she didn't get any of Janet's dressing. It was all gone too soon, and she had her mouth set for some of that dressing. Oh well, you couldn't get everything, but everybody tried.

Watermelon and melon tables were the first to run out. That didn't matter; everyone switched to the fruit tables.

But the dessert tables were next. The first victims were the sweet potato pies and the peach cobblers. Next all the other cobblers. But soon all the other desserts were gone too.

"Who made those sweet rolls? Those were real good."

"I wish I could get the recipe for the finger rolls. Those rolls were good too."

"And did you see all that bread. I just love homemade bread, but who has time to do it?"

And so the comments went all afternoon. Not only did they enjoy the good food, but they exchanged recipes, food, good fun and friendship

Everybody had dined sufficiently, or had ate until they were full, and all of the food was gone. A lot of people have been hoping to take something home with them. Now all they could take home were small pieces of one tid-bit or another and happy memories. But there were a few hot dogs left.

### The Eagles have landed with a THUD

Ahhh, after a good meal, what the body wants is a good nap. Most folks were feeling sleepy. You would see a person standing, sitting and talking, then in an instance they were stretched out on a bench or blanket. Some would be under trees, and others had straw hats over their faces. They were hoping to sleep.

Now, most of the kids were running and playing games. But there are always some children that cannot stand for mommy and daddy to rest. They always had to ask for something. Those were the ones that it made it difficult for parents to show love, but they did.

Everybody was relaxing and having fun. Children were playing games; grown ups were sleeping, talking, and playing cards and relaxing.

"Naw, naw, come on. Get up. It ain't gonna do you no good pretending to be sleepy. You know it is now time for some tail kickin' yours," called out Ethel.

"Woman, you just asking for it. Well we're gonna tan your behinds and put an end to all that nonsense y'all been talking about," yelled back Damon.

It was now time for the highlight event of the day, the big game. The women's softball team had challenged the men's baseball team, the Saginaw Eagles, to a fast pitch softball game.

The men had laughed and said, "You must be kidding. You ladies wouldn't stand a chance. We don't want to embarrass you."

And the ladies replied, "Embarrass us; please do."

So you know there had to be a game. After all, the men could not let this challenge go unanswered. If only for no other reason than some of them had to sleep with some of those women—and would never get any peace or sleep if they ignored the challenge.

Well now is the time for the big game. The ladies were on the field warming up. Only a few of the men were on the field getting loose. That's why Ethel was rousing the other men.

Slowly the rest of the Eagles took to the field. This was kind of embarrassing, trying to play a woman's team in a serious game. Some of the guys just couldn't get with it. Some had borrowed their kids softball gloves because they didn't want to mess up the pocket in their regular baseball glove.

The women ballplayers were in full dress uniform, with baseball cleats and all. The men were wearing only blue jeans and sweatshirts and baseball cleats—no uniform. They wanted to keep their uniforms clean because tomorrow they had a real game.

Well, that nothing game turned out to be quite a learning experience for the men. They learned that the shorter distance between the pitching mound and the batter's box made quite a difference in the timing.

They learned that that fat softball could curve, and they had to learn how to hit a curve ball all over again.

Mr. Eightball, Superman, and some others had been telling the team that the women were no pushovers and could play some ball. But male pride made most of them refuse to believe women could even play on their level—let alone think about beatin' a men's team. Well like I said, they did learn.

Superman struck out three times.

Eightball couldn't hit the ball far enough for him to hobble to first base. He couldn't even make a sacrifice bunt.

Johnny couldn't get the ball over the plate, and when he did, the ladies couldn't doing anything except hit it all over and out of the field.

You can imagine how Mr. Louis felt after the game. He was the base stealing leader of the Eagles. Yet, he was thrown out trying to steal second base against the ladies. And what was even more embarrassing, he was picked off first base by one of the oldest tricks in the book.

After the pitcher throws to first base to hold a runner, the first baseman pretended to throw the ball back to the pitcher. The keyword here is "pretended." She didn't throw the ball back, and Mr. Louis fell for it. Indeed it was a good game, and the women soundly beat the men. Bragging rights for that weekend belonged to the women.

As evening approached, the little ones were totally exhausted from a full day's fun and food. Mommy and Daddy carried the little sleepy angels with heads on their shoulders to the cars, gently placed them on the back seat, and returned to clean up and pick up more things.

Some people were staying and were lighting smoke fires to keep mosquitoes away.

So the day came to an end.

There were combined church Bible school and Sunday school picnics. However, I don't know if there were ever an openly public, joint picnic between the church folks, the street folks, and the sporting life folks.

Thus, while there were many Bay City Highway picnics, there was never really any Bay City Highway Picnic like this one—but there should have been one. It would have meant so much to the kids and even the grown folks.

It would have been fun in the summer of '49.

It would have been nice to remember.

# WENONAH BEACH

Whoppe, oopps, there goes something.
Wheeeeew, this is great. There goes something else.
Yipppeee......I really dig this. This is fun.
This is funnnnn,.......my foot!

What am I doing here? I must be out of my mind , if not now, I soon will be. I don't like this. This is not my idea of fun.

Rule number one—if your feet are solidly rooted on terra ferma, concrete sidewalks, or plain old dirt, why go crazy by getting on a contraption designed to make you loose your cotton candy, hot dog and mind? That thing, being a roller coaster.

Oh the rule, if you are on solid ground, stay there.

Now Carlton would like this. He searches out roller coasters and thrill rides on every vacation. I didn't discover this side of him until he visited us while I was toiling away on this book. I also found out that he can and loves to talk. All of us who grew up with him, remember him as being quiet. Boy, we never knew him or else he changed a lot. The truth is probably a lot of both.

But when I heard him say that he wanted go sky diving—and this was after he had been retired for few years—and that he planned to take a helicopter ride over the Grand Canyon. I wanted to know who was this guy, and what had he done to the Carlton I knew? Because this could not be the kid I grew up with. I knew him well.

His father had been choir director at our church and had been my best and toughest singing teacher. Mr. Carl DeGroat was a very talented man and a very close friend of mine and the family. So you see, I thought I really knew his son.

But back to the story. I do not like heights. High places do not agree with me; despite the fact that I worked five years on bridge construction to overcome my fear of heights.

However, when I was 11 years old, I didn't like anything tall, except girls. Short guys always liked tall girls. I don't know why. Tall girls always got sick of being bugged by short guys. I don't know why. But on with the fun of our story.

We're going to spend one Saturday afternoon at our two favorite parks on Saginaw Bay, the State Park and an amusement park called Wenonah Beach. These were picnic places, fishing places, family and kids playing places, and all in all, they were really fun places to go.

Nola Ruth and I were enduring the summer school Bible circuit, and this picnic was with the Catholic Church. My mother made certain we were busy in Bible schools all summer long. We were Catholics, and then we moved to the Baptist and Methodists schools, or any other schools that she could find.

But when the Catholic Church, like all the churches, went on a picnic, they took all the kids in the neighborhood anyway—whether they were Catholics or not. So it didn't matter that the Baptist, and others, went along with the Catholics.

The morning started out with me scrambling to find my swimsuit, a couple of extra tee-shirts, and maybe an extra pair of socks. And like always, I was missing a tennis shoe. By the time I located my lost shoe, I was running late as usual.

We arrived at the church just as they were loading the busses. Normally it was a school bus; sometimes they got a Greyhound bus or in our part of the state, a bus company known as Indian Trails. We'd put our bags in the storage area of the buses and find a place to sit. We settled back and tried to behave ourselves, like nice little children as we took this 20 or 30 mile trip to Wenonah Beach.

There was laughing and talking. Some were reading comic books, making jokes on each other, or were staring out the windows. Nobody would dare try to sleep. We were too young to know the value of sleep at that time.

The bus made its way up Bay City Highway. We passed the skating rink, Parkway Arena, owned by Mr. Braggs, one our social and local businessman. Mr. Braggs sponsored many local and national entertainers at this place.

Farther on the highway, we'd pass the Veterans Memorial, where we had many picnics. Oh, how can we forget the first place we passed, the muskrat farm. Yes, we actually had a place to farm muskrats. The fur was used for coats and trim, and from time to time, people would even eat them. In fact, our family had muskrat dinners. They tasted like coon, which, no matter what anybody said, did not taste like chicken. Of course as you well know, anything else seasoned and cooked right tastes like chicken.

Along the highway there were other little picnic areas. We passed fishing bait shops and just before you entered Bay City, a little local airport. Of course, we thought it was a big airport. To most of us, it was about the only airport we had ever seen, up to that point in time. You could take flying lessons, but who had money to take flying lessons.

You are now in Bay City (the other city by the bay). You drive up the main street, and even though it is a wide street, it is covered with a canopy of tall elms, golden oaks, and magnificent maples. Their branches are so big that when dressed in full leafage, they block out most of the sunlight even on the brightest of days...allowing the sun dominance only at intersections of big streets. This was nature's honor guard and with its attendants of lilac bushes, birch and various evergreen trees, they shielded us, as our Indian Trails coach turned and twisted along the city streets. In some places, the streets were following actual ancient Indian trails that were leading us to edge of the bay.

I, like many others, never knew the names of the streets that took us to the beaches. You learned by just watching as some one drove. So you got to know the way by feeling it and by the stores and houses where you made a left or right turn. I suppose there were signs directing you to the parks, but no one ever took the time to read or understand them. Then the next thing you knew, you were at the bay and the beach.

We pulled into the State Park because there were no admission fees. Unloading the busload of kids was orderly and calmly carried out. If you believe that, there is a lake for sale just across the road in front of my desert home.

Yes, there was an attempt to organize things as the children got off the bus. Notice I said "an attempt" but it never really happened. The kids grabbed their bags, their blankets, and towels and ran for the beach or to a picnic table. Plopping all their belongings on the picnic tables or in the sand, they immediately started finding something to get into.

Meanwhile, the grown ups were getting things together. They got the charcoal fires going, the hot dogs cooking, and the buns warming up. They made big tubs of Kool-Aid and passed out potato chips. Sometimes they would have the big 5 gallon cans of them, and at other times we had little bags of chips. There was penny candy, ice cream bars and cups, and popsicles.

After filling our little stomachs with all that good junk food, everyone was very cautious about allowing us to swim immediately after eating. So if we couldn't get in the water right away, what did we do instead if we were in State Park?

### Wenonah Beach

We begged and scrounged up rides to go to Wenonah Beach. So therefore, we did not get cramps from swimming; we ended up with upset stomachs from riding all the carnival rides and the roller coaster. This was the other beach situated on Saginaw Bay, right next to the State Park.

Wenonah Beach was a summer amusement park with all the various rides, like a merry-go-round, bumper cars, ferris wheel, loop to loops, and carnival-type midway games and shows.

But the pride of the park was a wooden frame roller coaster. I don't know if it had a name. This may have been before they started naming these stomach-turning, tracks of terror. Ooh oh, my wife just informed me that it was known as the "Jack Rabbit"(once again, the recall abilities of the writer are shown to be as sharp as a serving spoon).

This was one rickety thing that rocked, back and forth, and up-and-down, and made you feel like you were going to fall out at every bump, twist and turn. You felt that any minute it was gonna rock off the tracks, and in a split second, you'd see your whole life pass in front of your eyes because that would be the end of your world.

I did not want to go on the monster, but all the other kids were going; and besides some of the girls were going too. I couldn't let the girls know that I was chicken. I should have shown my wings and tail feathers.

The ride starts out harmless enough. They put this crusher bar across your lap to hold you in. And you grab the bar. It was only about a dozen people that started up the steep incline. Slowly the click, clack, and clink of the wheels and tracks and chains starts you moving. You can feel the car being towed by the chain as it goes up the first and steepest and longest incline; groaning and pulling the roller coaster car inches upward. Then, there is silence. There is nothing. The car seems to be hanging in space, standing still.

Then it slowly starts down the other side of the hill, and that's when all of your cotton candy breaks loose from the paper cone you refused to leave behind with Marvin. The car plunges down the other side faster than a speeding bullet...and with a lot less accuracy.

The car is rocking as it goes. Greater and wilder it rolls as it just about rolls off the track. Oopps, there goes somebody's hot dog, the one they were holding inside of them. You go up another incline and plunge down again; but this time you go into a sharp turn either to the right or the left. It doesn't matter, you are frightened. I mean really scared out of your mind.

Up-and-down and twisting, your hands clench the safety bar and then down and out you go. Your mouth is open trying to scream, trying to yell, but no sound comes out. Will this torture ever end? And just when you think that you can take no more, and that you're going to share your last candied apple with the people behind you, the ride comes to end thankfully!

While that was fun, I'm not gonna do it again. I'll take the Ferris wheel, cable cars or bumper cars, but no more roller coasters. That lasted until my children tricked me in taking them on one at Cedar Point in Sandusky, Ohio. I foolishly, trying to be a good father, took them on a shaky roller coaster. The next time they went my eldest daughter took her younger brother and sister on the roller coaster; and daddy, me, has never gotten on a roller coaster again.

One game where I always lost my pennies was the one with the little wooden circles where you'd try to throw around the top of pop bottles. I always came close and almost, but never quite, got it. I knew just one more chance, and this time I'd make it. And one more time the kid lost. I hated losing my money. So therefore, I knew I would never become a gambler.

But what is the beach without going swimming, without getting in the water? What is a beach without sagging, swimming trunks and wet tennis shoes? How can you not have sandy toes, soggy sandwiches, and sand in you kool-aid—that is if you are at the beach?

It really didn't matter if you were a good swimmer or not; just playing in the water, building sand castles, and watching the waves come along and wash the sand castles away was the fun.

Running up-and-down the beach, throwing water on the girls, or running away when they tried to throw water on you, was the "you're it" game to play.

Wenonah Beach and the State Park were our answers to Waikiki or Long Beach or Malibu. They were just as much fun and real to us as those other places. They were our places in the sun. And when we got older and were allowed to drive, they also became our little romantic rendezvous places

But at 11 years old, who was thinking about rendezvous and singing romantic songs? Well, I wasn't. Here again, I was a little slow.

Sooner or later, we'd get in the water and build our sand castles and come out of the water shivering and lie down on a towel on the hot sand to warm up. Then we'd be busy brushing the sand off after it's dried, many times on someone else. The girls were very careful not to get any sand in their hair, and the boys were kinda careful.

The sand would be hot underneath your feet, and you'd walk gingerly over the hot beach trying to find the tennis shoes you threw on the ground somewhere. Then as fast as you could, you put them on to save the bottom of your feet.

Naturally after the swimming, it was time to go get something to eat again. So there was more hot dogs and fried chicken and sandwiches. But let's not forgot roasting marshmallows on the grill.

Can you ever forget putting the marshmallows on the end of a stick and holding them over the charcoal until they were burned black on the outside and gooey on the inside. That was so good, and you had the stuff dripping all over the place. Marshmallows only tasted good when they were burnt. I wouldn't mind having a good old-fashioned one again.

And before you know, it was time to go home. The boys would go into the public change areas or anywhere hidden, to put on, hopefully, what were dry clothes. They didn't have any. The only thing dry was the sand, and it was everywhere.

The girls changed whereever it was proper and protected. We all helped clean up the area and climbed back into the buses to go home. And this time, on the way back, we did sleep.

After having a full day of fun and sun, I guess that's what being at the State Park and Wenonah Beach did to young kids, in the summer of '49.

I still remember.

# PART TWO

# BASEBALL
## THE FEEL AND ESSENCE
## OF THE GAME

# THE STATUS OF THE GAME

Anyway, in the summer of '49, there were picnics, hot dogs, hot tamales and bar-b-que. And then there was baseball. In the summer of '49, there was only one sport that counted...and that was baseball. Summer meant seeing lots and lots of baseball and many of the Negro Major Leagues teams: the Detroit Stars, the Birmingham Black Barons, the Chicago Black Sox, the Kansas City Monarchs, Indianapolis Clowns, and so on. The Negro leagues were still hanging on; although player integration into the white major leagues was beginning to affect the crowds, and the Negro fans were slowly turning their attention to the few blacks that were in the white major leagues. Eventually the Negro leagues died with too few chronicled memories.

But a small part of the Negro Major Leagues and the American Major Leagues came together at one of our houses on Farwell Street. They are the reasons that I became a life long Cleveland Indian's fan. During their travels through the midwest, the second black baseball player to play in the white major leagues, and a future team mate of his, at different times, lived with us.

Yes, Saginaw was a temporary home to both "Larry Doby" and

Luke Easter, who played first base for the Indians. Larry Doby was the Jackie Robinson of the American League. The league that history showed to be the much harder league, in which to break the color barrier.

However, integration had not yet taken its final death toll on Negro baseball.

There was one odd team that was important to the Negro league games in those days. Oh, how could I forget this team? This was one odd and strange looking team. They were strange looking in those days and would be so, even today. Yes they were the opposition for the Negro league teams, and guys were no pushovers. They played some mean (meaning good), hard and for real gut bucket baseball. They were pretty good.

Who were they? Well, this one strange, unofficial team of the Negro Major League teams, at least in Michigan, was a team of strong, big, strapling, full face covering bearded, religious, white men and boys from Benton Harbor, Michigan, known as "The House of David."

They provided the opposition when the local Negro teams and the Negro Major League teams toured the small towns of Michigan. And when the flyers said "The House of David" was going to play, everybody black and white knew that was going to be one good, clean (no cussin' and name callin') hard played game.

Yes, those bearded boys came to play some serious ball. The whole town turned out for these games because the goal of the day was to beat the Negro teams, especially the Negro Major League teams. Yet the Negro Major League teams almost always won; because this was their livin' and many times if they lost, they got little or no money.

And whereever the Negro teams went, Grandma and Momma were sure to follow. Many times the teams had to come back to Saginaw to sleep, and many times some players stayed at our house. So we got into the games free, and most of the time I was their bat boy.

When the movie "Bingo Long and His Traveling All-Stars" came out, I took my children to see what Negro baseball used to be and how it died. I told them that I was too young to know it, but as a bat boy for the Chicago Black Sox and other Negro Major League teams in Apena and around the state, I was watching and acting out a very small, non-speaking bit part in the big crowd scene in the death of a part of Americana. Too bad America never got to know those teams.

Yes, baseball still had some kind of magic about it. Everybody loved watching a good ball game. Of course you wanted your team to win, but if it was a good, fair, and a half-way clean game—not too much name calling, cussin' and so on—you could still go home feeling good.

Baseball didn't change your day to day life, but all in all, there was nothing like it that the whole family could enjoy. Momma could yell and call the ump a blind bat. Little sister could say "yeah" in agreement and boo. The boys could act like the men and pretend to be cussing under their breath, while yelling out loud other little pleasantries. And the men were pretty much careful about using profanity and cussing around the women and kids.

Ball players and men always had a big wad of chawin' tobacco in their mouth; disfiguring their jaw with an uneven lump and swelling that jaw to twice it's normal size. Next came the "look." That twisting of the head, with keenly intent and focused eyes, searching to the left, the right, behind him, in front of him, for the perfect or at least, an acceptable spot to spit!

With that look, he always found the right spot to hit with a mouthful of brown and odorific expectorant. Next, came the ritual of casually clawing and digging the surrounding dirt or gravel, with his sharp steel cleats—and just as non-chanlantly covering up the evidence of his excretion. The little boys just stuffed their jaws with bubble gum and never could quite get the spittin' part right.

The game of baseball was still king of all sports.

The Negro Major Leagues were in a hospice, waiting for the end.

But they didn't know that in the summer of '49.

I still remember.

# THE BALL PARK

## Slick's Farm

"What are you talking about, bratty?" I asked my sister, who at the moment was trying to be mysterious.

"It will cost you a quarter," she cryptically replied.

"A quarter for what?" I demanded

"For me not to tell Momma that you did not stay for the devotional services and prayers at church this morning. You missed the deacons and Brother Boone praying.

"You are wrong, you big story teller. But what if I didn't stay, what is it to you?" I asked.

"It's worth a quarter to me, for me not to tell Momma on you," chided my sister.

"I ain't got no time for playing around with you; you ain't getting' any money from me," and I started to walk away.

"I know that you went down to Chicken's Pool Hall with Jr., Thurman, Harold and some other boys and played pool instead of being at church.

"We did not," I shouted back.

"If I tell Momma you can't go to the game," she jeered.

"I did go to church, and I'm not paying you anything," I said indignantly

"You know the rule. If you don't go to church, you can't go to the show or ball game. And I'm telling if you don't pay me," said the heartless brat.

"And even if I was at Chicken's, I wouldn't pay you any money. That's blackmail," I said.

"Call it what you want, but it will still cost you a quarter for me not to tell on you," said Nola Ruth.

I was in a tight situation. If Momma knew about the pool hall, I'd be grounded. I had to bluff my way out of this. Besides I didn't have a quarter to give her.

"Momma, Mickey skipped church today," said the informer.

"Nola Ruth, I don't have time for this now. Get ready, so we can go to the game. I'll take care of Mickey later. The Birmingham Black Barons are playing today, and I want you kids to see them. We will be following them up north this week, and some of them might be staying with us for a night or two. So change your clothes and eat and let's go," said Momma.

So we piled into the car and headed for Slick's Farm, the home field of the Saginaw Eagles. The farm was in Carrollton, Michigan, and the easiest way to get there was crossing the Sixth Street Bridge. This was the most exciting part of the trip. It was an old, narrow bridge with wooden planks. Two cars could barely pass each other when meeting. It was a nerve racking ride because the Saginaw River was a good quarter to a half mile wide.

After driving over some winding dusty roads, you got to Slick's Farm and turned into a pasture. It had bleachers on both sides and something going for a ball field in the middle. It is only in retrospect that the field is described disparagingly. At that time we thought it was a great field.

There were benches beside the base lines that were the dugouts for the players. The bleachers were just that, plain bleachers. There were no box seats, reserved seats, or corporate booths—just plain, wooden, splintered bleachers. They were about six or eight rows high and pretty much wrapped around from first base to third base.

Up the hill, back by the road was a farmhouse, where they played a jukebox, held dances and so on. And next to the farm house were bar-b-que pits and a row or half circle of number two tubs, where that down home, cooked-up-north barbecue was teasing and pleasing everyone who smelled the queing.

Also, on those tubs, they were smoking hot dogs, chicken, hot sausages and anything else they could get their hands on. Down by the field, there was a concession stand where they sold the barbecue and hot dogs with plenty of mustard, and all the other food. And next to the stand, was our famous number two wash tubs full of ice, pop, and beer.

And of course there were the vendors, the snow cone man, peanut man, and hot tamale man. Sometimes there was a man selling popciles, ice cream bars, and "drumstick" ice cream cones.

Do you remember popsicle stick houses? We used to make fans, triangles, and even houses with Popsicle sticks. I was never that ambitious. It was all I could do to make a decent fan and a little one, at that.

What I really want to talk about was those drumsticks. I believe it was at Slick's Farm, one Sunday afternoon , where I saw my first drumstick ice cream cone. It was a thing of beauty. In your hand you careful grasped the cone. What they called a cake cone. Adorning that waffle cone was the scoop of ice cream smothered in chocolate. And the chocolate had a golden crown of crushed peanuts. I badly wanted one. I begged and begged; and finally, mother bought me one. That's one of the very few times my begging paid off.

It was as good as I had imagined that it would be. I never had too many drumsticks because they were not allowed within my budget. I don't remember how much they cost, but they were more than I could afford.

I don't remember the game that day. I think it was one of the better games that we played all season. I believe we won too. That's how much that drumstick affected my memory.

Slick's Farm was another one of those real fun family places. You'd have several hundred people there, and everybody was all laughing, joking, and just plain having a good time. Amazingly, would you believe it because women and children were about, you heard no swearing or cussin'. Profanity was just not socially acceptable in public.

You could do a lot of people watching at Slick's Farm too. For the most part, it was clean and done openly, nothing secretive at all. With the bright light of day, shining on everyone, there was nothing you could hide.

My most unforgettable memory at Slick's Farm was the time I was so intent on getting the bat, after a base hit, that I was walking to the plate to pick up the bat, just as Superman was rounding third base and barreling down on the catcher at home plate. Superman gently, as gently as he could going full speed, picked me up in one arm and swung me out-of-the-way, never letting go of me, and was still safe. As for me, I was a lot more careful after that.

Yep, Slick's Farm was what summer was all about: baseball, hot dogs, hot tamales, peanuts, popsicles, and drumsticks; and fans on edge to see another home run, gulping pop and beer by the gallons. All the while kids were running around pretending we were baseball players. But still the stomach pleasing highlight of the day was when Momma or somebody would allow you to have one or two bones of them good, mouth watering, barbecue cooked on those number two wash tubs.

You know, baseball and barbecue were kings in the summer of '49.

I still remember.

# AROUND THE BASEBALL FIELD

"That's where I wanted to play. You always play second base," I yelled.

"You play where I tell you or you don't play," said Harold.

Joe wanted to play third base and always ended up being the catcher. Me, I always wanted to play second base, but I always ended up in right field. Donny wanted to play shortstop and always ended up in right center field. Waterhead wanted to play third base too. But if Joe didn't catch and Gene didn't play third and Lionel, played center field, because Charlie Jones couldn't play, then Ezell B would play first and Clyde would play third, and Bo would play second. Pumpkin would play shortstop, and Water would have to catch, if he wanted to play, because he was from across the tracks anyway. Then Joe would play left center, and R.B. played deep, deep center, and Poop-a-dad played real center field, and if anybody was left over, he would play with me in right field. Oh yeah, everybody played. Sometimes, there'd be 12 guys on a team.

And that's the way it was when two guys wanted to play the same position. There was always one older guy that played that position last year. And if you wanted to play, you had to take whatever position was available to you, which meant I couldn't be the next Jackie Robinson and play second base, and Joe, more than he wanted to be, was the catcher and so on.

The older guys would say, "you play where I tell you to play or you don't play."

We also had our own designated hitter rule. A good hitter could pinch hit for younger kids or a real bad batter, and the bad hitter would run.

Now, it was not that I was a bad hitter, but Clyde Bennett and Roosevelt Barnes were better hitters, so in a tight game when it was my turn to bat, Clyde would say, "I'm hitting for you Mickey, you just run."

I guess that was a weird rule, but we never thought so. It was just the way we played ball. Still anyway, I always played right field.

### The Right Fielder

The loneliest man in the world is the right fielder. Well, maybe not the world but on the ball field, it's true. No body hits the ball to right field, unless it happens to be a weirdo, who is left handed or some one hits late—and by accident the ball ends up in right field. Although some guys thought they were good enough to pull a pitch and hit it where they wanted to, they were not that good.

Now you take the right fielder, he must keep up a constant chatter to keep from going to sleep. He gets more chances catching grounders and fly balls during warm up, than he will get in a month of games.

For real baseball players, despite the inactivity, it is not difficult to keep their minds in the game. But for me, just as in playing cards, my mind does things like contemplate about the true value of having only apple trees or plum and peach trees in ones back yard.

Sometimes I would think about how many enemy planes I'd shoot down, when I became a pilot. I guess you could say that my mind wandered, from time to time.

Sometimes, I would try and catch flying grasshoppers with my baseball mitt. Then, there was the time that I found a real four-leaf clover.

And it was always interesting to watch the women's softball team practice. And while watching the women's softball team practice, I would wonder why all the girls in our classes had such skinny legs. Little did I know that one day, a lot of those legs would be a lot bigger than we would want to talk about

You could do a lot of things while playing right field. So therefore, right field was the only safe position for me to play.

There's a hit

"Charlie, it's a hit. Get it," yelled the team.

"I got it. I got it," I yelled.

"Naw, I got it. Get out the way," as the second baseman caught it.

"That was my ball," I shouted.

"You were playing too far back," said the second baseman, Bo.

"But I could've got it," I said.

"You started running backwards, like you was scared of the ball," snickered Bo.

"I was not. I thought it was hit harder at first, but I changed direction and was getting' ready to catch the ball, when you jumped in front of me," I shouted back.

"Mickey, you were still 50 feet away when I caught the ball," truth stretcher Bo chided.

"I was not. Bo you can sure tell 'em. (And even now, to this day, he can still tell 'em.)

I did not play right field like Mr. Louis.

### *Mr. Louis vs. Right Field*

Mr. Louis played right field for the Saginaw Eagles, and he was very much apart of the game. He was all into the game every second of the game. He kept up the chatter. He encouraged his teammates. He talked about the other teams. He heckled batters of the other teams constantly. He'd encourage our pitcher on.

"He can't hit."

"The fool can't hit his way out of a wet paper bag."

"He can't hit the side of a barn, even if he's standing on it."

"The ump must be blind as a bat. Wait till nightfall then he can see."

He was a baseball player through and through. And could he field! He could cover right field and right center field like nobody else. He was so good that many times, he backed up the second baseman.

At the crack of the bat, any ball hit in his direction was considered dead meat (that's probably the wrong kind of metaphor). However, at the crack of the bat, any ball hit right of second base would be in his territory.

With smooth strides, he'd camp under the ball, waiting for it to make that stinging smack in the glove. And with a seamless fluid motion in grabbing the ball from the glove, swinging his left leg forward, and cocking the ball behind his ear along side his head, he'd fire the ball back to the infield.

And he had a rifle for a throwing arm. Oh so many fools thought they could advance from first to second or even third to home, on a fly ball to right; only to find the second baseman or shortstop, picking their teeth, while waiting for the witless clod who thought he could run on Louis.

And the catcher, in full face mask and padding, would be crouching 10 feet up the line, salivating, spitting tobacco juice between the bars of his mask. Hungry and eager, he was waiting to put a real hurtin' on this fool, who was dumb enuff' to run on my man Louis. This hit would make his whole week.

Boy oh boy, Mr. Louis could fire that ball. All of the teams in central Michigan knew not to mess with Mr. Louis. That's at least one area in life where he got his propers, his respect.

Poetry in motion it was, for Mickey, that big eyed, 11 year old me, to watch Mr. Louis in right field.

### The Catcher

If right field was the loneliest position in baseball, then catcher had to be the most gregarious, talkative, get in-your-face and personal business, and mess with your mind position on the field.

The catcher gives the pitcher the sign of what pitch to throw.

It's also the catcher's job to help position the infielders and outfielders on how to play certain batters. After playing a team for so many years, everybody knew just about what every team was capable of and what were the weaknesses of each batter. The catcher also knew how to get under the skin of everybody. Yes, the right fielder was all by itself, but the catcher had too much company.

If you are the pitcher, the catcher was always running out to go over the pitching signs, because you were getting them wrong or the other team was stealing them. And sometimes the catcher needed to get up and walk off a leg cramp. Anyway, he always ended those pitching mound conferences by trying to calm you down. Of course the catcher was never sorry for insisting that you throw a slow curve to the last batter, which he parked somewhere over the left field fence. Yes the catcher was always setting the pitcher straight.

If you were the opposing batter, the catcher was always trying to do something to distract you like:

*Your shoes are untied;*
*You know you can't hit him;*
*I hear you were two sheets in the wind last night;*
*Was that you had drank so much that you lost two sheets in the wind;*
*What's it like getting drunk?*
*Don't look now but he's about to pitch? Swing batter.*
*Why do you try to play this game?*
*Better look out your left foot's too far in the batter's box.*
*You think you really know how to play this game?*
*That was strike three. I told you, you couldn't hit off him, but nooo, you wouldn't listen.*

The next batter got variations of the same. The chatter would go on and after the batter struck out, the catcher's parting words of wisdom might be:

*I told you to ask somebody if you didn't know what you were doing.*
*Mr. Umpire, please give us a break. We know you want the other team to win, but at least give us half a chance. That was a strike, can't you see?*
*I hear you're back on afternoons, Willie. You must've really made somebody mad. Man what did you do?*
*I hear you got more seniority than those foundry bricks and cupolas.*
*That was strike two. Man you just can't see.*

The batter and the umpire were not just taking this chatter in stride. They were giving it back to the catcher, just as well as he was giving it to them. They had some real interesting and lively arguments or conversations going on, but every time the pitcher delivered the ball to the plate, all paid attention to that ball.  The batter wanted to knock the cover off the ball.  The umpire wanted to call it a ball or a strike.  And the catcher's job was to make each ball look like it was a strike.

Of course, these conversations were only heard by the batter, the umpire, and maybe some people directly behind home plate.  It was never a loud conversation, just loud enough to distract the batter.  And  sometimes so low the batter would have to strain hear.

### The First Baseman

First base is the second hot corner on the field, because every ball hit in the infield comes to you.  Not as a perfect throw but thrown to the left, to the right, high or low.  But you've gotta make them look good.  Normally you are expected to be a good hitter, which was the case with Superman and Mr. Eightball.  The only problem, as mentioned before, Eightball could not run.  He had to hit a double to get a single.  But he did know how to milk a pitcher and get a walk.  He got more walks than anybody.

The first baseman was almost as popular as the catcher.  But if the game was going well, no one stayed around to talk to him.

Superman and Eight Ball played first base for the Saginaw Eagles.  Superman was lean, strong and muscular.  Whereas, Mr. Eightball was long, lean, lanky and slow, very slow.  They brought different skills to the position.  They both had their long stretch.  I think Mr. Eightball's was longer, but it was not as graceful, captivating, or energetic as Superman's.

If you were the runner stuck on first base when Eightball was playing, you might decide to take a lead off first base and discover that you couldn't go anywhere.  Eightball would be holding your pants. Of course, the umpire would get on him about it. He would say that he's sorry, but he'd do it again.  He was always doing that trick of pretending to throw the ball back to the pitcher after a pick off throw.  Everybody knew—and the whole State of Michigan knew—that Eightball would try to play that trick, at least six times a game.  But at least once a game, he would get some fool out.  And that fool would be the laughing stock of the fans, but his teammates would  be slightly miffed.

Also, when you're on first base, Eightball or Superman would talk to you just like the catcher did at home plate:

*You got drunk last night?*

*Are you feet hurting or those shoes too tight?*

*You guys have bus trouble getting to the game?*

*I hear you got a new car. I'd sure like to see it and get a ride.*

*You'd better watch this pitcher, he's very good at picking guys off, but you're too smart to get caught.*

And so the chatter would go.

I never wanted to play first base. But it was a good position. I can't remember who always wanted to play first base, but Clyde and Roosevelt Barnes played it a lot.

### Second Baseman

Well I never got to play second base much because two other guys were better than I was. Second base was just about as far as my throwing arm allowed me to throw. I was a good fielder. I studied my fundamentals very well, but I was not a very good hitter. So I never got to play second base as much as I wanted

Since it became obvious that I was never going to be another Jackie Robinson, I decided to become a fighter pilot. As you can see that has nothing to do with playing baseball, so that's why I was stuck in right field.

At second base, you do a lot of running around backing up the shortstop at second base; backing up for first baseman; playing in short right field; short right-center field; short center field and coming in to field bunts. It's a pretty active and a good position. I liked the position.

### The Shortstop

The in-between Man. To me, next to second base, the best position on the infield was shortstop. There is a ball hit in the hole between second and third. Deep in the hole the shortstop races, spears the ball back handed, turns in mid air, and throws a strike to first base—and the runner is out. There is pure, raw poetry in motion, watching the shortstop. He has to be able to go his left, go to his right. He's got to cover second base, back up third base, and he's got to have a good throwing arm.

Playing second base and shortstop, while you're on the field, the only chatter that you can do is yell at the batter, encourage the pitcher, and make the umpire mad. But believe me the game definitely comes to you. You are always a part of the game.

### Third Base. What Was I Thinking Of?

Baseball fans call it the hot corner.

You've got to know when to leave well enough alone.

It's like one of those things where your eyes are bigger than your stomach.

I must have been out my Oklahoma Okee Fa-noke mind.

I must have been out to lunch.

It must've been something in my cereal that morning, because even my sister, said I was acting strange.

This is what happened. When I got to the play field, Clyde, Water and even Gene were not there. So I jumped up and said, I wanted to play third base.

Now, I had never really played third base before with the full team and all, but since I was a good fielder, I figured I could handle the job. I was just tired of falling asleep in right field. Like I said, I was a pretty good fielder, and I knew I could handle that aspect of the game. What I did not know is that the name, hot corner, is well deserved. I also discovered a few things about my throwing arm, which we will get into later.

Some of the guys tried to talk me out of it, but I insisted. Now I could really be into the game. I could be in on every play. I could keep my mind in the game.

So let the game(s) begin.

Now the first batter up hits a hard ball down my way, and before I could move, in self-defense, my glove instinctively found a way to protect my certain vital parts, necessary for me to have a chance at having descendants. The ball smacked into the glove, stinging the devil out of my hand. I was more surprised that anyone that I caught ball.

ball popped out of my glove and luckily into my throwing

hand, and I wound up and threw the ball. It almost made it to first, on the first bounce. But it took a bounce and one half, but the runner was out.

"Way to go Mickey," everybody on the team shouted.

I pretended like it was nothing. Like I didn't understand why they were so surprised.

The next ball is hit in the gap between shortstop and third. I gave it "that I'm gonna be a hero try" but I couldn't come up it. But I looked good, stretching out, and taking a mouthful of dirt.

"That's OK. We'll get two this time," the team said.

With the next batter, my house of cards started to tumble. This time I was playing even with the bag; another ball was hit my way. I cleanly fielded the ball. I was determined to get the ball to first base without a bounce.

And I did so, phenomenally. I got the ball to first base, to the first base players' bench, and on into the street. It really wasn't a bad throw; the first baseman just wasn't nine feet tall. But it was good the ball went into the street, because it meant the runner could only advance one base, instead of two bases.

There was the name calling and grumbling after that play. I just sucked it up and said, the ball got away from me, that's all

Come the next batter, and more cards fall. He hits a slow ground ball; and despite all the lessons we had about fielding grounders, getting down in front of them, blocking the ball, I let the ball go right between my legs.

There was nothing to do, but withstand comments of my teammates and ridicule of the other team and fans. Pulling my cap down over my eyes and crouching more to ground, determined not to make another mistake, I dared em' to hit another ball my way.

The next ball was hit, again to third base. Didn't they hit the ball anywhere else? What happened to all of those fly balls to left field? Anyway it was a perfect double play ball. All I had to do was field it and toss it underhanded to the shortstop at second base, who would then throw to first.

Ever mindful of my last over thrown ball, I was determined not to make that mistake again. This time I made it just a light, easy toss to the shortstop. But it was too easy. The ball did not reach second base and the shortstop.

The bases were loaded, and I guess it was my fault. I was really into the game now. My house of cards was almost completely down. The wheels were almost all the way off the cart. My goose was just about cooked . I was about to be ridden out of town on a rail. You get the picture. I was not doing too good at third base.

And another ball was hit to third base. I again fielded the ball cleanly, and stepped on the bag, making a forced out. Just as I stepped on the bag, the runner stepped on my foot. I screamed in pain. No, make that yelled in pain; boys don't scream. I fell to the ground and grabbed my foot; and I gamely stood up.

All of the team came running around, shouting, "Are you okay, Mickey?"

"It's just a little something. I'll be okay," I said.

But I was not a complete dummy. I knew that it was time for me to quit third base.

I now knew personally, why they called it the hot corner. And that much baseball, I did not want.

Besides, by this time, Walter and Clyde had showed up, so I said, "Walter can play third base." I never asked to play third base again. You can keep third base.

Though I don't remember who played third base for the Saginaw Eagles, I do remember he was a good player. The Saginaw Eagles were a good team. They could play with anybody in the country. Back then as a kid growing up, you don't think much about just how good your teams were and how good the people you knew were.

These were your hard-working foundry men. They were working five and six days a week; eight to twelve hours a day; and playing baseball. Playing for nothing but the love of the game. They were playing heads up, toe to toe with some of the best players in the country. Saginaw people, black and white, were very lucky; because when the Negro Major League teams came to town, everybody who loved baseball came to watch them play. Little did we know then we were watching the end of an era.

Yep, that summer I learned to leave third base alone.

That too, was a good part of the summer of '49.


I still remember.

# CAPTURE THE MOMENT

Baseball is filled with moments of man-to-man encounters. They are moments when these two guys alone make the difference in the game. The pressure that gets the heart to pumping—that floods the body with extra adrenaline—is seen as strained muscles and clenched jaws and hands, and furrowed foreheads.

Moments like these don't happen in every game. And the truly great moments worth capturing are few. But the "Off-Broadway" not the greatest, but still good exciting plays could be seen at Slick's Farm just about every other Sunday. That's what made watching the Eagles play ball so great.

## The Runner and the Catcher

For instance there's a long fly ball hit to left-center field; it's off the fence. The runner at second has only one thought—he's gonna head for home. He's gotta score, 'cause the game is on the line. The fans are screaming their heads off.

This is the kind of excitement, that special baseball moment, that I'm talkin' about. You see, there was nothing like watching a runner take a hard slide or barrel into a catcher in the ninth inning when the game was on the line.

There was nothing like the sound of a runner's steel cleats tearing at the corner of the bag as the runner rounds third base, heading for home.

There was nothing like the sound of the crowd roaring so much; it just fills the runner's head and ears until he can't even hear them anymore.

All he hears is the sound of his run down, worn, sharp and uneven cleats, clawing to dig into the base path and to take hold so that he doesn't slip or fall down.

All he hears is the crunch of his cleats as they dig into the sandy cinder and gravel base path that over time has become more rocks and gravel than sand and cinder.

All he hears is the sound of scrapping rocks and grinding pebbles on a base path filled with pock holes and little ridges that cause each stride to twist and wobble.

All he hears is the smack of the ball, as it hits in the glove of the cutoff man knowing that the throw to the plate is on its way.

All he hears is his labored inhaling and exhaling gulps of air for breath, knowing that the throw will probably beat him to the plate, and it's going to be him and the catcher, man-to-man, and he doesn't plan on losing.

All he hears is his team yelling for him to slide.

All he hears is the scrape of rock, gravel of the base path as his cleats and the whole right side of his body starts his slide.

All he hears is the clash of the crash of him and the catcher colliding.

All he hears is their grunting and the smack of their bodies and the whoosh of the breath forced from their lungs, out through flared nostrils and clenched teeth.

Then for a split second he hears nothing. Then the roar of the crowd is heard again; loud and deafening, too loud to hear words.

All he can do is look for the ump. And he sees the ump with both arms stretched out sideways.

And now all he can hear is his own voice shouting and yellin' safe, safe, safe.

Such was baseball. In the summer of '49 there was no other game, period.

I still remember.

## You Must Not Steal

The Bible book of Exodus, Chapter 20 verse 16 reads. "You must not steal."(nwt) That is true everywhere except in baseball. What was a game of baseball without Louis stealing second base. That's Mr. Louis. Now it's true that his bat was not that great, but once he got on base. Look out.

Take for example this particular Sunday. The Saginaw Eagles were playing a team out of Owosso, Michigan. And the home team was not doing that great. In fact, they were behind by a couple runs, and it was now the bottom of the ninth inning.

Then, Two-Way-George came to the plate and hit an off speed pitch to right field. He ended up on first. Next up, was Eight Ball. Eight Ball was a tall, lanky guy that could not run. He was so slow that Nola Ruth could run backwards and beat him to first base. But, he was a good sacrifice man. So he layed down a perfect bunt and advanced Two-Way-George to second base.

Willie McGee got a hold of a pitch that looked like it was going all the way, but ended up being a long fly ball out to straight away center field.

Two-Way-George moved to third.

Then, next up was Louis. He crouched at the plate and waited for the first pitch. It was low and outside, ball one. The next pitch, a hard fast one was right down the middle, where Louis looked at it and let it go by.

"Strike one," yelled the umpire.

The next pitch was a hard slider on the inside and jammed him up tight.

"Ball two," yelled the umpire.

Louis glared at the pitcher. He stepped out of the batter's box. Looked down at the third base coach. He scoops up some dirt and rubs it on his hands. He walks around a bit and steps back in the batter's box. He wiggles around as all batters always do and sets his footing.

The pitcher glares back and silently mouthed a few choice words to Louis. There was no love or brotherhood between Saginaw "first warders" and guys from Owosso. The gall of that little foundry worker, this little guy, thinking he could hit his stuff.

The wind up, the pitch. A low fast ball.

"Ball three," shouts the ump.

The fans were getting excited.

"A walk is as good as a hit Louis," the stands yelled.

"Get on base Louis," some other fans chanted.

Louis stepped out of the box again, looked at the third base coach, then the first base coach and at last into the dugout. He stepped back in the box. Squirms and sets his feet. Then stares at the pitcher and swings his bat easily back and forth waiting for the pitch.

Then the pitcher steps off the mound. He picks up the rosin bag and turns to look at the outfield. He steps back on the mound. He shakes off the catcher's first sign. All pitchers do it. He nods at the second sign. He goes into a stretch and checks Two-Way-George at third. He delivers. Louis is taking all the way. The pitch is right down the middle.

"Strike two," snaps the ump.

It's a full count. There is two out in the inning. Louis represents the tying run. So here comes the next pitch.

"Ball four," yells the ump.

The whole Owosso dugout jumps to their feet in protest and tell the ump that he was blind, and a few other things.

Louis takes first base. The objective now is don't let Louis steal second base. That way they'll still have a chance at a force out to get out of the inning. But everybody in central Michigan knows that Louis was gonna try to steal second base, and Superman comes to the plate.

And so, the cat and mouse game begins. The pitcher goes into a stretch, looks over his shoulder toward Louis at first base, pretends he's gonna throw to the plate, turns back to the mound, and in a quick spin fires the ball to first base. Louis gets back to first, well before the sneak attack throw.

Pitcher goes into a stretch again, glances at Louis, then at Superman, and glances back at Louis; then he delivers the pitch to the plate.

Strike one. Who cares, everybody's watching Louis at first. The catcher fires the ball back to the first baseman, hoping to catch Louis off guard, but Louis, wise to this old trick and the catcher, isn't fooled. He stepped back on the bag nonchalantly and smiled at the catcher.

Yes indeed, Louis was wise to this trick.

The pitcher goes into a stretch again. He looks over his shoulder at Louis again. Louis takes a big lead at first base. The pitcher steps off the mound and looks back to first base. Louis walks back to first base. The pitcher steps back on the mound, goes into a stretch, steps off the rubber, wheels and throws to first hoping to catch Louis, taking too big of a lead, off guard. But Louis gets back safely.

The fans start taunting the pitcher. "Go on and pitch. You know you cain't do nothin' with him."

The pitcher steps to the mound again. He picks up the rosin bag. He goes into a stretch. Louis takes another big lead, and the pitcher delivers a called ball to home plate. Louis had taken off for second. Right away, the catcher comes up, throwing to second. But Louis had faked them out of their sweat socks. He wasn't going anywhere. So he walks calmly back to first base.

The fans are laughing and having a good time, pointing at the pitcher, playing with the catcher, and laughing at everybody on the field.

The umpire calls time; turns his back to the pitcher's mound, and taking a whisk broom from his back pocket, brushes off home plate. A ritual done quite frequently in the old days.

The umpire finishes and yells, "play ball."

Louis takes another big lead. The pitcher checks him back to the bag. The pitcher goes into the stretch; Louis takes another big lead. The pitcher delivers the ball to the plate, and this time he does go. Louis had waited till the pitcher had given away that tell-tale sign that this pitch was going to take a second longer to deliver. There was always something that the pitcher or catcher did that told a base-stealing thief like Louis, when to head for second.

The batter swings at an outside pitch; the catcher comes up with the ball and throws to second. The pitcher ducks out of the way, as a ball sails over his head. Louis starts a hook slide, around to the center field side of the base. The second baseman catches the ball and makes a wide sweeping swing. A movement that he knows will ensure a clean tag. He did all of the proper things to tag Louis...and misses.

"Safe," yells, the ump.

The fans go wild, and Two-Way-George breaks for home and slides in safely.

Yep, that was fun to watch. Louis was just too good on the bases. This too was part of baseball in the summer of '49.

I still remember.

# The Pitcher and the Batter

If you want tension and drama and unforgettable moments, well check this out. This is another element or ingredient of the essence of baseball.

It was Sunday afternoon at Slick's Farm. The game was on the line. It was the ninth inning, two outs with one more to get. The Saginaw Eagles had been behind by two runs, but now for the first time, they led by one run. However, there was a runner at second and the winning run at the plate. But the count that mattered, at that moment, was two balls and two strikes.

The batter is pawing at the dirt in the batter's box. He steps to the plate, takes his stance, raises his bat and cocks it just behind his ear, and gets ready for that fast ball he knows the pitcher Johnny Bryant is going to throw.

The pitcher, as they always do, shakes off the catcher's first sign. He checks the runner, at second. He starts his stretch. Then he wheels and turns, and fires the ball toward the bag, and the second baseman, who saw the pitcher's silent signal, makes the catch...and in one unbroken sweeping motion, tags the surprised runner as he slides head first back to the bag.

"Safe," yells the umpire, and the whole crowd rises and shouts in protest.

The batter, once again, goes through his ritual. This time the pitcher digs at the pitching mound, making the batter so nervous that he steps out of the box again.

While the drama between the pitcher and batter was being played, the fans in the stands were advising and encouraging the Eagles, the home team. But they were yelling things, other than encouragement, to the other team. The fans were also letting the pitcher know that the batter did not possess very impressive batting skills.

"He can't hit his way out of a wet paper bag," yelled one proper looking lady.

"You'd better roll it to him, that's the only way he's gonna hit it," barked out one man somewhere in the middle of the stands.

"Batter, batter, batter, swing! Wait 'til he throws the ball," yells the crowd.

"Come on, baby, you can get him," yelled a group of teenage girls to the handsome Mr. Bryant.

"Easy out. Easy out. Easy out," came from some boys behind the players on the bench.

It had been a long and hard game. Mr. Johnny had gone all the way. The sun was hot. Sweat was running down his forehead into his eyes. He was constantly wiping away the sweat. He was tired, but he wasn't gonna let anybody know. Tired arm, sweaty face, or aching hip was not getting him out of this game. There was too much of him on that field.

Redbone, the catcher, was again calling for a low outside curve. He shook it off, but Redbone flashed the sign again. Mr. Johnny hated that pitch this late in the game with his arm being so tired. However, Redbone felt it was his safest pitch because his arm was tired.

Mr. Johnny stepped off the mound and pulled his handkerchief from his back pocket. He looked around and taking off his cap, he wiped his face. It was just a gesture to wipe off the running sweat. There was no wiping your face dry, because he was wringing sweat out his handkerchief. He looked up to the sky, shielding his eyes with his glove hand, he said to himself that it was even too hot for the birds to fly.

Why in the devil does Redbone keep calling for that pitch. It made him mad. Oh well, he knew Redbone was trying to help his arm because that big German Frank at the plate could park that ball into the middle of next week, if Johnny's fast ball was just a little bit high or slow.

OK, so here goes. Mr. Johnny tuns back to the mound. He picks up the rosin bag. He again gets the same sign from the catcher. He accepts it this time. He steps on the rubber, starts his stretch, and checks the runner at second. He delivers. Uh oh, it's in the dirt.

Redbone jumps, scrambles to his knees to block the wayward pitch and to keep the runner from stealing third.

Mr. Johnny glares at Redbone. He knew he shouldn't have tried that curve 'cause his control wasn't good enough at this point in the game. Now he was really mad. This game was too close to be trying that pitch now. He kept on glaring at the catcher. Redbone, sheepishly, looked away.

Again Mr. Johnny took his time; only now it was to get his temper under control. He turned back to the plate, and the catcher started flashing signs. He shook them all off. He was now seething and steaming. He spits through clenched teeth.

Redbone gets up and starts toward the mound. But Mr. Johnny vigorously waves him back.

The count was 3 to 2, and he was tired. But he'll be darned if he was gonna let Frank beat him. It was do or die time,

If they do it in the movies and if Satchel Paige does it, well for once, it was his time to do it. He figured he had about four or five good pitches left or one great pitch. So what the heck, here goes.

He turns and motions and yells to the outfielders to come on into the edge of the infield. Mr. Johnny motioned for the infielders to go to their bases.

They all just looked at him with a crook in their neck and wondered what in the sam-hill was he doing. But he kept on waving them into the infield and to their bases.

So the outfielders came in, and the infielders went to their bags and just stood there. The poor shortstop didn't know what to do. Then he turned and grinned at big Frank, the batter.

The other team and Frank were dumbfounded

"What were those colored boys doing?" they wondered.

"Frank'll tear the cover off that ball for sure now. Why Frank will murder the bum and the ball," they said among themselves.

"They can't insult us like that and get away with it," they spat out in anger.

"Kill him Frank," the whole team yelled.

Now the fans were into it, and they were going wild.

"Johnny! What are you doing, Honey?" screamed Miss Ophelia.

"You can get him," shouted Momma.

Men and kids were whistling and stomping their feet so much that it felt like the stands were going to collapse. Yes the fans were going wild; at least on the Eagles side of the field.

On the other side of the field, the Owosso side, the fans sat in stunned frozen silence. Their mouths were open. They could not understand the wild commotion of the colored fans. It just didn't make any sense. What were they doing? They must be crazy.

Now, the pitcher just ignored the runner at second and went into a full wind up. Everybody in the ballpark gasped. They were wide eyed and had their mouth's open. Their hot dogs stopped in mid flight on the way to open mouths. Mothers clutched their infants, and little boys strained to look around daddy's legs or belly. It seemed as though the world paused, because everybody knew what was coming next. It was gonna be smokin' heat, nothin' but pure mean, eye to eye, man to man, in yo' face, smokin' heat.

"Now pay attention, look close son; you may never see this again," said one daddy to his son.

The pitcher had gone into a full wind up. There was still a man on base. The other team's best hitter was at the plate. And the pitcher was letting it all hang out.

Look, Eightball, the first baseman, had walked over and sat on the ump's bench. The crowd was laughing and eating it up.

The batter began to feel a tingle. He too knew what was coming. He tried to concentrate. But this was his big test too. He felt the weight of his team on his bat. He dug in more and crouched lower in the batter's box.

Then he signals the ump for time and steps out of the box. He takes a deep breath and looks down at the third base coach. He bends over and picks up some dirt and rubs the sweat off his hands. He looks at Mr. Johnny and grins. They both know it'll be all over the plant tomorrow whatever happens now. He'll be a hero or a joke.

He steps back in the batter's box. His fingers flex and regrips the bat tighter, as he rocks easy, back and forth on the balls of his feet, waiting, just waiting. His eyes are straining, squinting to catch the earliest look possible, when the pitcher releases the ball.

Here comes the pitch. The pitcher unwinds, and all the metaphors written before about the quickness of the uncoiling of a Cobra as it lunges; the speed of lightin' versus the speed of an ordinary pitch; the delivery of the piston like arm; these and more all apply.

Because on that day, at that moment, Mr. Johnny reached down, I mean really deep inside and came up with something. Yes, it had smoke. It was smokin' and it was fire. It was a fire like lightning. It was like white blinding light. Mr. Johnny wound up, twisted his body, kicked that leg, and let that ball explode from the end of his arm.

The poor batter never saw it. He was still looking at the pitcher when he heard something hard hit the catcher's glove. Frank had a look of stunned bewilderment on his face.

On the other side of the field, his teammates were staring with their mouths open, first looking at the pitcher and then the catcher, wondering if this was some sort of trick. But then a loud yell snapped them back to reality.

"Strike three, yourrrr out," the umpire yelled.

Frank never stood a chance; after all he was only human and that pitch was something else. The batter's teammates tried to console him. But, in this one fight, toe to toe, the batter had lost. The pitcher had won. It was that simple. It was beautiful and pure baseball.

And in the summer of '49, baseball was the only sport. Period!

I still remember.

## Superman The Home Run King

"That ball's hit hard. The right fielder is going back, back, but he won't get this one. That ball is outta' here," yelled Mr. Cal, who was working the loud speakers this week. He had his own way of saying, "that ball is outta' here!"

Hitting home runs. Say what you want, but that's the most exciting thing in baseball. That's what the game is all about. Sure there are other great plays, pitching and fielding and so on. But those all happen because they were trying to keep the guy at the plate from hitting a home run.

Everybody wants to see a home run everytime somebody comes up to the plate. You can hit 350, be a great ballplayer in the field, but if you don't hit home runs, you're just another ball player. Now you can be a lousy infielder or outfielder, but if you hit home runs to any degree above average, you will get more press, popularity or money than the rest of the team.

Youngsters, women and homeowners, smile and joke with him wherever he goes by. He can walk down the street and every kid in the neighborhood wants his autograph. That's just the way the game is.

Well, the Saginaw Eagles had one man like that, and they called him Superman. Superman played first base. Every now and then he played third. Sometimes he even caught. But he was at his best on first base.

His stretch was a thing of beauty, as he scooped up a hard throw from the third baseman. Or it could be the shortstop, after making a terrific stop on a ball hit deep in the hole, throwing across the infield. Then Superman would do a split stretch to get the runner. How he could stretch.

Superman was a well-built guy with big shoulders, flat waist, arms and biceps like building columns. He was a hard swinging guy and always swung for the fences. But sometimes he played it smart. He knew when to just get on base or connect with the ball to move a runner along. He was a team player that happened to hit a lot of home runs.

Let's pick it up again with the snapshot of Louis, still at first base. Now guess who's the next batter up? It is Superman, representing the winning run. The one guy the Owosso team did not want to face at this point in time.

The Owosso team manager called time. He, the catcher, and third baseman walked to the pitcher's mound. They were arguing about whether or not to pitch to Superman. They knew he was dangerous. If he got a hold of one, the game was over. But the next batter was Willie McGhee. Willie had bad feet and couldn't run either. Although he can't run, he's a decent hitter.

But the pitcher believed his arm was still strong. He felt he could get Superman out. And since he was the team's best pitcher and had got them this far already, the manager let him stay in and pitch to Superman.

When the fans saw Superman walk towards the plate, they went wild. OK, so now Superman stepped in the batter's box. He goes into the batter's grunt and grind, you know, that little ritual that all batters go through.

Meanwhile on the mound, the pitcher, looking to the outfield, repositioned the fielders and had them play deeper. He turns towards the plate. He goes into his stretch, and he checks Louis at first.

Now we are about to witness, two cat and mouse games. One game is with the pitcher and Louis, and other game is between the pitcher and Superman. And the big question was, could the pitcher play two cat and mouse games at once and win either of them and the ball game too.

In the "You Should Not Steal" snapshot we know the pitcher lost that game.

When it got to be two strikes on Superman with Louis on second, the manager once again called time out to talk to the pitcher. He said with a hit, Louis could maybe score from second, tying the game. On the other hand, with first base open still, just walk Superman, and maybe Willie would hit into a force out, and the inning would be over. Still the pitcher wanted a piece of Superman (that was his macho pride actin' grown).

It didn't take long to find the answer to the burning issue of game number two. As the pitcher cocked his leg and started his delivery to home plate, he let fly a really bad pitch. It was low and outside. But Superman went after it like it was his last bologna sandwich, and he hadn't eaten in 3-½ days.

He teed off on that ball that was almost in the dirt, and when that baseball tee shot connected, it sounded like a rifle shot going off next to your ear. The fans jumped to their feet. Hot dogs, hot tamales, and bar-b-que were knocked from hands, beer was spilled, and even chawin' tobacco wads were swallowed.

There may have been no joy in Mudville, because when Casey came to bat, Casey struck out...too bad. But at Slick's Farm, and that evening up and down Sixth and Washington Streets and on Potter Street, there was not only joy, but there was partying and a heap of good times.

You see Superman had shown those farmers something. He had hit that ball so hard, that some say it didn't come down for a day and a half. Superman had not struck out. Superman had hit a home run.

That was baseball in '49. The best game, period.

I still remember.

## THE SUMMER IS OVER
## THIS IS THE LAST HOORAY

The summer is almost over, oh well, for us kids that means it's almost time for school again. The County Fair opens in another couple weeks. And up in northern Michigan, the nights are already cool. The leaves are beginning to turn red, yellow, orange, purple and brown, and all those startling brilliant colors that say the summer party is over. This changing of the guards of color makes Michigan one of the most beautiful states in the country at this time of year.

We have had barbecue galore, hot dogs and hot tamales and even taco parties. We have indeed ate well this summer.

Me, Marvin, Freddie, Willie Jeff and Uncle Albert have chased rabbits and squirrels, foxes and fooled around at the muskrat farm.

We've chased girls with bugs snakes and with nothing but for the fun of it because they let us.

We've wandered through corn fields and ate fresh corn off the stalk right there in the field. I have ate so many crab apples that I feel like one.

And the first ward and across the tracks guys have done things together or to each other, all summer long.

There was little Eddie who lives around the corner on Norman Street, who followed us around all summer and didn't get in the way too much. Then there were Joe and Buddy who got along with everybody.

I can't think of everything we did, but it was indeed a fun-filled summer.

And just as I told you, there were ever so many hot dogs, til they were coming out of your ears.

There were street vendors such as the peanut man, snow cone man, and the hot tamale man who made the rounds on Potter Street, Sixth Street, and at the baseball games.

There were fish fries and fried chicken parties.

Oh, did I tell you about that there was fishing.

Gees, I hope that I didn't forget to tell you that there was baseball.

And most important and enjoyable of all is that there was barbecue cooked on number two wash tubs.

And just because summer was over, the people watching on Potter Street didn't stop. We did it in the winter too. After all, Potter Street was still the street life, the happening street; it was our downtown street.

I really didn't know what snapshots to take from my family album of memories for this summer of '49. I just started talking to me, myself, and I, and the book just seemed to happen.

My friends and acquaintances will question why I didn't talk about this or that. They will tell me about stories that I missed, and about people I forgot. And I will be most definitely told that I remembered it all wrong, and it didn't happen that way.

But it was the last summer of our innocence. It was the last time that Blacks could believe that individual achievement alone would let one have a piece of the American apple pie. But despite personal tragedies and losses, we still hopefully looked towards a good future life.

### *Discovery*

The summer of '49 was a time of discovery.

I discovered the world outside of Saginaw.

I discovered the mystical, eerie quality that Spanish moss gives to the roadside as we traveled the back roads of Louisiana.

I discovered how the setting of the sun on a Mississippi dirt road plunged you into total darkness, filling your mind with fear and making your senses acute. Making them tender, like sand paper rubbed on your skin and how that darkness made you alert, attentive and reactive. You sense how your whole body strains, eager to hear the next sound; to see the reflection of the eyes of some creature on the side of the road; then watch a firefly flitter on and off and disappear. When you get away from the city, nightfall means total darkness. The moon and the stars take on a different and added significance. They are no longer merely optical beauties there in the sky. They are now the candles to your foot path. Stars mark your direction; hopefully, you are on the right path.

I discovered the gaudiness and the bright lights of the French Quarter in New Orleans. It is now more than a picture postcard or a story in a magazine. The city that is under the sea is alive, kicking and for real. The big muddy Mississippi brings commerce, new life, and sad tales to "Naw'lens" everyday.

And always there was fishing.

And everywhere we went on that long trip, there was discovery. There was new discovery for Grandma and Uncle Alex. There were memories and always a question of "I wonder what happened to so and so? You know. They used to live up by past the sawmill, right up from old man Willie John."

Then there was the pain of discovering that a friend had died, and they didn't know it.

Did you know that in '49 or '50, the drinking water in Racine, Wisconsin, was crystal clear, ice cold and sweet. It tasted like no other city water. And yes, there was a cute little girl that I met and we wrote for about a year. I don't remember her name, but she was a very sweet little girl

And can you imagine the wonder of the joy of discovery that Uncle Alex and Grandma felt in finding a lost brother and a new city. That city became my new home, Ft. Wayne, Indiana. I knew little about the social fabric or climate of that town in 1949 or '50. I merely met other people who were friendly, and we became friends.

I discovered that the hills and mountains of Kentucky and Tennessee have their own kind of beauty; the misty cloudy halos that encircle the peaks and obscure the depth of the valleys are beautiful. But if I can help it, I'll never drive on those twisting, narrow, two-lane mountain roads again.

Then there was the state of Georgia. "Sweet and Brown, and always on my mind" with that dried, dusty red clay and Alabama was just like Georgia. Both states were covered in southern yellow pines everywhere you go.

Wherever we went, we were always anxious to see how each town was different. However, "people" were the most interesting discoveries. I noticed new people thought we were different and sometimes weird—just as we thought they were different and some of them were really wierd.

And always there was fishing, barbecue, hot dogs, baseball and more fishing everywhere. There was never enough time to get it all done.

But the most important thing I learned that summer was never to fight another girl, always leave yourself running room. There was also the discovery that maybe there was more to girls than I had thought of before, but I still didn't know what. As I said before, I was slow.

I became an official observer during those years. I always wanted to be around other people and enjoy them, but I really didn't care to fully participate. After all, as kids, we were supposedly to be seen and not heard. Well I saw little bit, but Nola Ruth saw a lot and heard a lot more.

Every Sunday there was Sunday school and church, Sunday dinner, and the baseball game at Slick's Farm or on the road somewhere else. The dinner was most of the time fried chicken, (no one was concerned about cholesterol and all that stuff in those days), and whatever else Momma fixed.

But the highlight of every of every weekend was the Sunday baseball game. Two or three hundred people from around the area brought the kids, picnic baskets, fruit jars and Kool-Aid and watched the local heroes play anyone that dared to challenge them.

## The Last Hooray

And the highlight of that summer was when our beloved Saginaw Eagles played the Kansas City Monarchs, the Negro Major League Champions. The Sunday crowd was two or three times bigger than at other times. After all, the Monarchs were in town. It was not the first time that they played the Saginaw Eagles, and most of the time they beat us. Those guys played ball five days a week. They made a living at it. Every now and then our guys would beat them or another major league team.

That Sunday, in September, had everybody in town talking. Traffic along the Sixth Street bridge was scary. Yes, the famous, the great Kansas City Monarchs were going to play our Saginaw Eagles. And just as every Sunday I was gonna be the bat boy. I didn't know much, but I knew that this was a special game.

**I do remember.**

The game indeed was a special game. It was a good game. I don't remember the details of the game. The only thing I know is that the Saginaw Eagles played well.

I don't know how many hot dogs or cups of Kool-Aid I had.

I don't know if Momma and Miss Ophelia talked about the umpire more than they talked about the other players.

I do remember that I had never seen so many people at Slick's Farm before.

I do remember the sun was hot and bright, and you had to shade your eyes from the glare.

I do remember that Mr. Louis stole second base on the Kansas City Monarchs.

I do remember Mr. Johnny pitched his heart out and that the Kansas City Monarchs had more of him than they wanted.

I do remember that Mr. Eightball got THREE walks, cause that was the only way he was gonna get on base.

I do remember that Mr. Superman hit a home run; the only score of the game.

I do remember that the Saginaw Eagles played well!

I do remember that when the game was over, all of Saginaw, black, white, and Mexican were happy, happy, happy. Potter Street was jumping. Sixth Street was just filled.

The Cabana and/or El Charros' (my historical source, my wife, tells me it was not the Cabana in '49), the Mexican Beer gardens, Charlie's Beer Garden (I always liked the name of that bar) and Johnny

Williams' Beer Garden were all jumping. The jukeboxes were blasting; people were dancing, and drinks were flowing.

I do remember passing houses and porches all over town, and people were laughing and shouting with beer or Kool-Aid in one hand and chicken in the other.

Yes indeed, it was a beautiful summer. There could be no finer ending to the summer than the fact that the Kansas City Monarchs, the Negro Major League National Champions, were defeated that year by our local heroes.

Indeed, the Saginaw Eagles played well at the end of the summer in 1949.

And always there was fishing in "The Summer of '49."

HOW FONDLY I REMEMBER

All those wonderful things about,

## "THE SUMMER OF '49 –
## HOT DOGS, HOT TAMALES AND
## NUMBER TWO TUBS"

*Lois Louise Brewer Brewster at the age of 62.*
*Showing off at Nola Ruth's Cadillac.*

*All of Momma's Grandchildren. She was proud of them all.*
*They also were shielded from and survived Grandma.*
*Chantale Esther Bothuell; Rose-Anesta Bothuell; Philip Lamont*
*Sangster; Lenore Estelle Sangster; Charlie Bothuell IV.*

twice a day

Printed in the United States
48191LVS00003BA/106-126

9 780971 095472